124   LXXVI. Inter genera ruborum rhamnos appellatur
a Graecis candidior, fruticosior et[1] ramos spargens
rectis aculeis, non ut ceteri aduncis, foliis maioribus.
alterum genus eius silvestre, nigrius et quadamtenus
rubens, fert veluti folliculos. huius radice decocta in
aqua fit medicamentum quod vocatur lycium.
semen secundas trahit. ille autem candidior ad-
stringit magis refrigerat, collectionibus et vulneribus adcommodatior. folia utriusque et cruda et
decocta inlinuntur cum oleo.

125   LXXVII. Lycium praestantius spina fieri tradunt
quam et pyxacanthon chironian[a] vocant, qualem in
Indicis arboribus diximus, quoniam longe praestan-
tissimum aestimatur Indicum.[b] coquuntur in aqua
tusi rami radicesque summae amaritudinis aereo vase
per triduum, serumque exempto ligno, donec mellis
crassitudo fiat. adulteratur amaris sucis, etiam

126   amurca et felle bubulo. spuma eius ac flos quidam
oculorum medicamentis reconditur. reliquo suco
faciem purgat et psoras sanat, erosos angulos oculorum veteresque fluctiones, aures purulentas, tonsillas,
gingivas, tussim, sanguinis excreationes fabae magni-
tudine devoratum aut, si ex vulneribus fluat, inlitum,
rhagadia, genitalium ulcera, adtritus, ulcera recentia
et serpentia ac putrescentia, in naribus clavos,
suppurationes. bibitur et mulieribus in lacte contra

[1] fruticosior et *plures codd.*; *Mayhoff*: frutex is floret X:
et fruticosior, is floret *Detlefsen, vulg.*

---

[a] From Chiron, the centaur who was credited with great
medical knowledge.
[b] See XII. § 31.

EYE OF NATURE

WALTER PHILLIPS GALLERY

CATALOGUING IN PUBLICATION DATA

Eye of Nature

Based on exhibitions held June 5 – July 10,
August 3 – September 17,
and November 12 – December 17, 1989
at the Walter Phillips Gallery
in Banff, Alberta.
ISBN 0-920159-46-X

1. Art, Canadian. 2. Art, American.
3. Art, Modern—20th century—Canada.
4. Art, Modern—20th century—United States.
5. Nature (Aesthetics) I. Augaitis, Daina.
II. Pakasaar, Helga. III. Walter Phillips Gallery.
N6545.E92 1991 709'.71'074712332 C91-091103-7

Introduction

Preserved pockets of natural environments are modern-day reminders of human alienation from nature. In Banff National Park, where the Walter Phillips Gallery is located, the striking surroundings create an atmosphere of heightened sensitivity to nature as object — parcelled, promoted, bartered and sold. Park boundaries draw the line where human interaction with nature begins. This division reveals the disjunction between industrial notions of social progress and human intimacy with nature.

In the postmodern era, however, notions of nature as object are changing. The widespread realization that nature has been alienated in Western social and cultural development has prompted a reconsideration of its significance. But the questions now are urgent, as environmental degradation escalates. We are left to deal with nature in our fabricated landscapes, left to look at its destruction reaching an almost crisis state. Contemporary artists examining social change are sensitive to the representation of nature as a cultural construction in their investigations of the power of nature and human attempts to control it. Our alienation from nature, the mediation of technology and the tendency to anthropomorphize elements of nature have all been critiqued.

This publication brings together a range of visual artists and writers who address concerns related to the *eye of nature*. This eye is a metaphor for the vision, illumination and knowledge of nature as a cultural construction. It is the "I" of human origins in nature, prior to technological alienation, and it is the eye that traces the development of Western culture and the creation and reflection of notions of nature over time. A number of artists who address these issues exhibited work at the Walter Phillips Gallery over the course of three exhibitions. This publication documents their work and builds on common themes through several essays and artist projects commissioned for the book.

With the work of Bill Viola and Laurie Walker, the exhibition *Eye of Nature I* focused on nature as a reflection of social consciousness. Viola's video installation uses nature as the symbolic origin for the technological age. Similarly, Walker's sculptures evoke analogies between natural and technological forms. The artist created endsheets for this publication based on one of her works in the exhibition. Jeffrey Spalding and Ritsuko Taho express alienation from nature in their "wish landscapes" exhibited in *Eye of Nature II*, the second of the two-part exhibition. Spalding's paintings flirt with the ideal while exerting an anxiety about this relationship. Taho, in her large-scale installation, presents an abstracted view of the Banff landscape expressing the transformative powers of nature. The third exhibition documented in this publication presented the work of Christina Kubisch whose audio installations comment on the manipulation of nature. In Banff, her indoor and outdoor installations were environments for engaged listening. The works of these artists are discussed in essays by Daina Augaitis, who curated *Eye of Nature I*, Helga Pakasaar, curator of *Eye of Nature II*, and Hans Dickel, a German writer whose essay on Christina Kubisch's work has been translated and adapted for this publication.

Additional points of view were invited from Canadian artists whose work has addressed similar concerns — Robert Fones, Rodney Graham, Carroll Moppett and Edward Poitras. Robert Fones' *Erratics Train* traces examples of what is largely perceived as displaced nature. From his sequence of photographs of glacial erratics unfold notions of the natural and belonging. Rodney Graham presents a series of six inverted trees photographed in Flanders, Belgium. Disrupting perceptions of "natural," these trees comment on symbolic understandings of nature. Carroll Moppett's project, *Dreamland,* focuses on nature as manipulated in the name of science. By reframing nature magazine images, she raises questions about control and abuse in light of the conventional view of progress. Using contrasts in text, Edward Poitras points to definitions of land, people and control. His project suggests complex relationships between colonial powers, indigenous peoples and the claiming of geographic and cultural space.

Accompanying these artworks are essays by David Garneau, Maureen Sherlock, Matthew Teitelbaum and Scott Watson. Garneau offers an analysis of Carroll Moppett's project and discusses the artist's concern with the dominance of nature and the pain inflicted by this system on a broad social level. Maureen Sherlock covers considerable territory in her survey of the philosophical underpinnings of particular contemporary art practices that relate to the politics of viewing nature. Colonial and postcolonial perceptions of nature and their expression in art are discussed in Matthew Teitelbaum's essay, focusing on Canadian art practice, including the work of Fones, Graham and Poitras. Like Teitelbaum, Scott Watson is concerned with oppressive representations of nature and the colonization of Canada, in particular the homophobia it engendered.

Collectively, the contributors to this publication offer a range of provocative views on the role of art in the interpretation and construction of notions of nature. We live in the world of the eye, the supremacy of visually mediated information dominating our lives. We skim the visual surface of things, storing information for later use when we can take time to analyze it. The exhibitions, essays and artist projects in this book represent that moment of looking beneath the surface.

SENTIENT NATURE

SEEING NATURE:
AND THE WORKS OF BILL VIOLA
AND LAURIE WALKER

Daina Augaitis

Neutrality is not one of the qualities of vision. "The eye is not a camera," Raymond Williams explained,

> or if it is a camera, it is a camera the results of which have to be developed. That development is by a human brain which of course has evolved over uncountable generations, but which at the same time is built up in our growth as children and towards maturity, by sets of rules from our society, from the relationships we are actually in. These rules to a large extent go on determining what we see and what we can describe.[1]

Thus our physical eyes comprise only part of a complex process of perception, calling on the mind's eye for cultural codes that inform the translation of data and symbols into meaning, changing an unintelligible world into one in which human beings can function. It is impossible to remember how, as infants, we learned to see. Similarly, it is difficult to understand changes in the codes for visual translation that have occurred over the centuries. For example, when the first natural historians attempted to chart their environments — mazes of natural phenomena that had not been enumerated — the authority of science alone did not dictate norms for determining what was significant and worth noting. Nor could hindsight draw on accumulated material for relative analyses in this cognitive process. Perception then, is appropriately referred to as "both foretaste and aftereffect in our physical and mental worlds,"[2] having the capacity of responding to and shaping ideas.

With its utilitarian perspective and growing emphasis on scientific quantification, the late eighteenth century brought numerous changes that implicated vision. Improvements in travel, for example, required that the eye adapt to a moving landscape through the frame of a vehicle window and learn new methods of composition at increasingly higher speeds. In his account of the history of perception, Don Gifford describes Henri Matisse's automobile rides through the Provençal landscape, during which the artist insisted on speeds no greater than five kilometres per hour in order to see his subject accurately, "otherwise you have no sense of the trees" as the "middle ground and horizon advance to lay claim to the eye."[3] Such changes in travel, along with other developments of industrialization, in turn

1. Raymond Williams, *Culture and Society* (Harmondsworth: Penguin, 1963), 21.

2. Don Gifford, *The Farther Shore – A Natural History of Perception*, 1798–1984 (New York: Vintage Books, 1991), 15.

3. Ibid., 30.

affected the mind's eye — the personal and social interpretations of visual stimuli. This increasing emphasis on a perspectival scopic regime[4] marked the transformation of the Western relationship with nature characterized by domination.

The cultural eye responded to a progression of optical devices such as the stereoscope, camera obscura and camera lucida, all of which reflected the world through a lens that altered and interpreted the properties of the image. Cameras and other such tools were usually heralded as inventions that would present truth and statistical exactitude. The shifts in what we saw and how we saw it were subtle at first; however, as our eyes extended outside our bodies to inhabit the technological space of various apparatuses, the subjectivity of sight became more apparent. And today, technologies that simulate virtual realities bring new and unknown challenges to cultural and physiological thresholds of perception, amplifying the subjective realm of human experience. With the aid of new communications media, the facts and fictions of what we see merge into a saturated blur.

Nature — the untampered physical environment — is read and perceived no differently than other mediated images that we encounter. After all, natural history is written through human history; descriptions of natural phenomena are filtered through scientific concepts and modified by contextualized analysis. Nature is invested with cultural meaning and does not elude fictional characterization. As the effects of industrialization cast a pall around the globe, Western cultures now seem to be recoiling from the tainted environment, craving an untampered nature and an immediate contact with it. Yet, for many of us, the practical and emotional understanding gained from intimate experiences in nature is fading since our urban environments no longer allow for such access or involvement. As nature plays a decreasing role in the lives of large urban populations, the vision of it begins to fracture and dissipate. Nature becomes an image imbued with longing and nostalgia but, simultaneously, it is pronounced as alien, described in relation to anthropomorphic concepts of machinery and information systems, relegated to the territory of the non-artificial. A longing for nature was once a longing for one's origins, but now these origins are increasingly distanced.

4. Martin Jay, "Scopic Regimes of Modernity" in *Vision and Visuality*, ed. Hal Foster (Seattle: Bay Press, 1988).

How then do we as individuals navigate this minefield of histories, codes and perceptions that separate us from our environment? Laurie Walker and Bill Viola each make their own forays into this territory, exploring these questions in their respective art practices. The works of both are commentaries on cultural perception and its place in contemporary society.

In the development of his video work, Bill Viola has sought to comprehend video technology and its mediating effect on the image. At the same time, he has immersed himself in the analysis of the viewing experience and the position of the viewer. In doing so, he has found it necessary to understand human perception, "not only how the camera works, but how the eye functions, and the ear, how the brain processes information...."[5] His installation, *Theater of Memory*, exhibited in *Eye of Nature I*, exemplifies his exploration of the metaphysical characterization of reality as a whole.

5. Raymond Bellour, "An Interview with Bill Viola," *October* 34 (Fall 1985), 94.

In *Theater of Memory* the viewer enters a dark cave-like room — the non-verbal timelessness of the subconscious — and finds a large uprooted tree lying on its side, lit only by small electric lanterns flickering on the tree's branches. A wind chime tinkles in the darkness, its delicate sounds intermittently superseded by loud and abrupt electronic crackles of static, as if to shock the mind and jolt it out of stasis. Beyond the tree is a wall-sized video screen on which a stream of television "snow" is projected; degenerated images sporadically come into focus. The images seem out of phase and out of sync with the human receptors that read them. Our eyes search for recognition as these moments of television, art and history flutter on and off the screen, in and out of memory. Rather than subdue the electronic static, as television viewers may attempt to do, Viola foregrounds it and questions how these properties of sound and image interfere with our perceptual processes. The artist's description of one of his own discoveries finds parallels in this installation:

> I remember reading about the brain and the central nervous system,
> trying to understand what causes the triggering of nerve firings that
> recreate patterns of past sensations, finally evoking a memory.

I came across the fact that all of the neurons in the brain are physically disconnected from each other, beginning and ending in a tiny
gap of empty space. The flickering pattern evoked by the tiny sparks
of thought bridging these gaps becomes the actual form and substance of our ideas. All of our thoughts have at their center this small
point of nothingness.[6]

Using non-verbal sound and archetypal images, Viola creates a stream of information that flows between the human conscious and subconscious levels. The experience enunciates the difficulty (sometimes resulting in paralysis) of discerning
images around us, and the work acknowledges the need to create room for self-
doubt and tentativeness in taking stock of these images and their interpretations.

The leafless tree is the counterpoint to the video projection. In many contexts, the
tree is interpreted as a symbol of life, knowledge and unity of the natural world. Here
the tree takes no nourishment, there are no fruits, and no leaves for protection. The
innocence of life's origins is uprooted. The installation is a convergence of the natural landscape with the psychological one, where imagination and cultural memory
join with the material of the environment. While Viola's work is concerned with the
investigation of life and being itself, it concomitantly questions the specifics of a relationship with nature and the structures that determine its meaning. The artist is influ-
enced by Eastern disciplines of mind and spiritual training, in which "the skill of the
master, for example, is considered to be not so much the accumulation of knowledge
or even the acute awareness of the present. Rather it is seen as the knowing of how a
present action will be transformed into the future."[7] For the artist, this is linked to
the concept of memory: "Memory is as much about the future as it is about the
past...it is another editing process. Memory is active."[8]

The mind's ongoing editing process occurs as a function of time — a critical dimension of Viola's work. Time operates on many axes in this installation: the eternal
time of nature is represented by the tree; the time of a civilization bursts through
images across the video screen; the time of the mind is revealed in split-second
shifts in the process of perception and merges with the real time of the viewer

6. *Bill Viola*, ed. Barbara London (New York: The
Museum of Modern Art, 1987), 55.

7. Bellour, 101.

8. Bellour, 103.

standing in the installation. All of these time frames converge in this work, saturating the mind during an extended exposure: Viola posits that "duration is to consciousness as light is to the eye." In an analysis of Viola's work, Gene Youngblood articulates these implications of time:

> Sustained duration forces thinking instead of only seeing: it's a metaphor for contemplation. It allows us to step outside of the event-stream [of cinema] and perceive it in a larger context of meaning and relationship....There's a necessity for a meditative time that allows us to project our imagination onto the event-stream. Only in this way can sensation become thought, perception become an art of intelligence and of grace. Only in this way does the process of viewing become a creative act. No longer voyeurs, we give the experience to ourselves. We become the narrative.[9]

For the viewer, self-constructed narratives may emerge in the after-experience of the artist's work as its dimensions are personalized and images of the inner mind are allowed to frame understandings of the outer world. This process of understanding truths from a personal position is an important one in Viola's work, and it reflects the ideas of William Blake who looked outward from the self to the larger external world. This approach is also true in the work of Laurie Walker, an artist who operates with similar assumptions. Both attempt, as Blake stated, "to know the world in a grain of sand," to explore the larger world as it is expressed in the minutae of life. Blake fought against the dominance of materialism that surrounded him in the eighteenth century, studying the material world not in the name of empirical observation, but to understand how it functioned as a series of symbols, behind which lay infinity. Both artists identify with Blake's interpretation and ordering of the world, using imagination and symbols freely in trying to relate the microscopic and macroscopic.

Laurie Walker's project explores perceptions that circulate between science, myth and nature. Her work exhibited in *Eye of Nature I* emerges from a metaphoric study of plants in which she presents the fragility of the most insignificant plant, and, in doing so, reflects on the larger cosmos: she points to the paradox of finding the universal in one's immediate surroundings.

9. Gene Youngblood, "Metaphysical Structuralism: The Videotapes of Bill Viola," *Millenium Film Journal* 20/21 (Fall/Winter 1988/89), 84.

Laurie Walker
False Solomon's Seal (Smilacina racemosa) 1988
drawing/sculpture installation
Photo: Centre de Documentation Yvan Boulerice

Laurie Walker
False Solomon's Seal (Smilacina racemosa) 1988
drawing/sculpture installation
Photo: Laurie Walker

The artist depicts four flowers with highly suggestive names — Common Ragweed, Venus Flytrap, False Solomon's Seal, Wandering Bower — in detailed botanical drawings accompanied by sculpture steeped in connotative associations. Her drawings appear to be objective analyses executed by a natural historian, but their three-dimensional counterparts project characteristics that implicate industrial and post-industrial societies as well as their mythological antecedents. Each of these works draws on layers of reference which entwine historically constructed notions of knowledge, authority and beauty with contemporary understandings of natural environments.

Wandering Bower (Solanum planetum) is rendered physically as a meticulously placed book on a wooden lectern. The book is quite rare — *Historia Naturalis* by Pliny the Elder — one of the first chronicles detailing an encyclopedic knowledge of the natural world. Berries have been brutally pressed between pages of the book, their blood-red juices staining the scientific text. The artwork delineates the moment of a violent unredemptive killing, as the plant is pressed into words and nature is subsumed into culture. The fiction of knowledge is further exemplified in the artist's scientific drawing of the plant. Seemingly anatomically correct, it is a fabrication, mocking the widespread indelible faith in science. Together, the falsified drawing and manipulated textbook speak aggressively about the transformation of previously held facts into modern day myth through the imposition of new information. The result is a provocation or destabilization of current systems of knowledge.

As a plant, *False Solomon's Seal (Smilacina racemosa)* might epitomize a victorious nature, buttressed by invisible forces. The plant exists as a rhyzome with an underground network of concentrated genetic material that can spring up and regenerate anywhere, each node encoding the entire history of the plant. Walker's sculptural equivalent is created from a series of four manhole covers, each with the emblematic imprint of a different city, emphasizing travel and progress. At the tip of the work is a scythe-shaped stem that seems to protrude from a manhole cover inscribed with a six-pointed star (the Star of David, which would have been Solomon's seal). Solomon was a Biblical figure, possessing powers of healing: the

Laurie Walker
Venus Flytrap (Dionaea muscipula) 1989
drawing/sculpture installation
Photo: Laurie Walker

10. Laurie Walker (M.F.A. paper, Nova Scotia College of Art and Design, 1987), 3.

plant too is known to have medicinal properties. However, manhole covers identify the city's underground network of putrid waste, a system with the potential to pollute and lethally infect. In Walker's sculpture, the tops of the manhole covers are sealed in red wax and the scythe has not dealt its final blow. The work suggests the inevitable has not yet occurred; the impenetrable wealth of the plant (and the sealed sewage of the city) is still intact, if only for the moment.

The artist tells of a Greek myth in which the fallen scythe was used by Kronos to castrate Uranus. As the severed genitals floated out to sea, they produced a white foam which gave birth to Venus. The *Venus Flytrap (Dionaea muscipula)* is another revenge of the plant world. Walker's sculpture, paralleling the artifice of the plant, consists of three enormous shovels from earth-moving machines joined together by a copper ring. An arrow is poised at its centre, ready to pounce on its prey, shoot off its seeds. Seduction figures prominently in the circle of opened cups, reflecting a range of possible desires, from sexual love to capitalist greed. The artist uses highly symbolic materials that conjure celestial love: copper is the metal linked to Venus, the goddess of love (often accompanied by Cupid with his arrow); the steel of the buckets is associated with Mars, the god of war. These symbols, used in astrology, botany and mythology, are combined here to form a hermaphroditic union of love and war, not unlike the current confused response to nature in Western cultures. Using animism as a tool, the artist imparts life-like attributes to inanimate objects as a "process of analogy and projection by which the inanimate becomes animate and therefore closer and more understandable."[10] Although animism is thought to be a primitive view of the world, perhaps now more than ever it is a concept worth considering. It is entirely human to implicate ourselves in whatever it is we try to understand: an awareness of this complicity disrupts the binary vision of subject and object that frames a widespread world view.

The courtship of Venus and Mars suggested in *Venus Flytrap* comments upon specific relationships used by ancients to interpret planetary movements from the images, patterns and hieroglyphs used as repositories for complex astronomical knowledge. Contemporary society is inclined to believe that linear quantification rather than

Laurie Walker
Venus Flytrap (Dionaea muscipula) 1989
drawing/sculpture installation
Photo: Monte Greenshields

pattern recognition of cosmology will accurately describe the natural environment. However, in Western culture, in spite of our emphasis on scientific developments, there remain as many ambiguities between illusion and objective reality as there may have been for the ancients. Current methods may not be that much more sophisticated, and it is Walker's intention to point out discrepancies between our perception of an image and the actual thing being represented. Like Viola, Walker believes that imagination has an important role to play in perception and that the process of perception is partly responsible for the creation of the phenomena that are observed.

Both artists in *Eye of Nature I* seek to bring imagination back into analyses of the world, to re-assess spiritual and mythological connections while considering how perception and knowledge operate in the larger sphere of cultural memory. The artists attempt to find personal understandings of the natural environment in a cultural milieu full of fragmented notions of self, other, identity, belonging and nature. From an individual standpoint, this quest offers a restorative approach to the making of meaning. While the search for universal truth is widely indicted in postmodern culture as an authoritative attempt to impose self-serving values, these artists invert this agenda to suggest that meaning is made within an individual context. From this strategic position, dualities imposed by universal truths are conflated and meaning remains intact.

The authority invested in vision relies on the distinction between subject and object. When these categories are collapsed through explorations of perception, as in the work of Bill Viola and Laurie Walker, the privileged position of the scopic regime of modernity is resisted. The resulting awareness of the visual process of interpretation described earlier by Raymond Williams opens opportunities for a re-assessment of previously held truths about the object, the subject and both the natural and material environments.

Bill Viola

Theater of Memory 1985
colour videotape projected on large screen, 30-foot
uprooted tree in dark room with 50 electric lanterns,
windchime, amplified stereo sound
7 x 9.45 m installation area
Collection: Newport Harbor Art Museum, California

Laurie Walker

False Solomon's Seal (Smilacina racemosa) 1988
watercolour on paper, cast iron, wax, scythe, chain
aquarelle painting: 89 x 69 cm
mixed media sculpture: 550 x 183 x 76 cm
Collection: Andrée and Patrice Drouin

Common Ragweed (Ambrosia artemisiifolia) 1989
watercolour on paper, graphite, cast iron, glass beads,
amber beads, plastic tubing, steel
aquarelle painting: 84 x 69 cm
mixed media sculpture: 132 x 117 x 60 cm
Collection: Michel Giroux

Venus Flytrap (Dionaea muscipula) 1989
watercolour on paper, steel, copper, wax
aquarelle painting: 84 x 64 cm
mixed media sculpture: 300 x 300 x 120 cm
Collection: Robert-Jean Chénier

Wandering Bower (Solanum planetum) 1989
watercolour on paper, book, glass, plant, wood
aquarelle painting: 87 x 67 cm
mixed media sculpture: 12 x 32 x 24 cm
Collection: René Bertrand

Nature and culture are often pitted at opposite poles in debates concerning technological advancement. How can technology, the argument goes, bridge the distance from nature that has been created by conventional terms of progress? Berlin artist Christina Kubisch attempts to reveal and conflate the gap through soundscapes — interactive audio installations — which implicate viewers in the making of meaning about nature, technology and human manipulation. In her first Canadian exhibition, Kubisch installed two audio works for the Walter Phillips Gallery, using both indoor and outdoor sites for reflection on the evocative overlap between natural and electronic sounds. In the context of earlier work, these landscapes of sound represent the artist's concerns that have developed over time. German writer Hans Dickel describes the artist's interests in an essay, "Orte der Zeit," translated in part below.

In her outdoor installations, Kubisch typically uses trees as picture carriers to give form in the outdoors to a network of suspended cables that serve as the source of artificial sound — sound which emanates from the cables for listeners wearing magnetically induced earphones. In the past, the artist has wrapped trees and shrubs in parks and forests with similarly coloured wires, resembling shackles around tree trunks, containers of plant energy, or electrocardiograms that listen to internal sounds and measure the pulse of life. When draped loosely around the tree tops though, they hang and spread as freely as natural branches. In the same way the cables follow the lines of the trees, sounds too are specially created for the location — natural sounds are recorded and synthetically transformed. While wire and sound clearly interact with nature in these outdoor installations, an artificial network strung in a thicket of overhanging branches has a very strange effect, like that of a technical apparatus being forced upon nature. By inventing a sound-producing cable, Kubisch emphasizes the possibility of reproducing sound, and yet, with the cable technique and its attendant line drawings, our attention is drawn back to natural phenomena. The relationship between electronic nature and natural electronics emerges as a central concern in Kubisch's work.

In contrast to the open air pieces — externally oriented "open works of art," to use

Umberto Eco's phrase — which require audience participation in order to be properly realized, the sound installations since 1984 have been produced in darkened interiors. They respond to the architectural particulars of a given exhibition space, attempting to trace its history and expose the secrets hidden in the walls. The first sound reliefs were conceived as murals to be listened to, with wires tracing elementary forms. In darkened rooms, black lights pick out the glowing, pigment-covered cables; they look like drawings, visually illustrating a given room — its history, atmosphere and architectural quality brought to expression through sound. But they also transform the space, allowing it to take on a new, unknown quality.

During this period, Kubisch prepared several wire constructions that filled up vast spaces through the immaterial constructions of sound fields on the wall as well as through perceptible, transparent architectural forms. In this way, Kubisch took a step not just from the outside to the inside, but also from the sound to the third dimension, from the wall into space. She created a sound installation in a neutral, right-angled space as part of the music and performance program of *documenta 8*, which distinctly brought to mind Russian constructivism of the 1920s. Spread like a fan, wires were attached to two separate supports in the central axis of the space, as though completing the oscillation of a wave. Here a "place of time" truly came into being; passages of time were converted into sculpture through which the visitor could walk. With their own movements, visitors could transform the sounds into musical movements. The listener becomes composer.

Kubisch's sound objects created since 1988 seem to take the experience of the encounter with nature and architecture and combine them in the form of independent sculptures. The transformation of these into autonomous creations is invested with a visual concentration where the works take on individual contours. Based on aesthetic distance, the pieces seem even less direct than the installations; instead, the acoustic aura is spread subversively throughout the space. The initial sense of disorientation can lead the viewer through to unusually intense experiences of perception.

Kubisch has, in a highly individual way, made the interrelationship between nature, humanity and technology the theme of her work, manifest in installations that are a combination of music and art, sound and picture, electronic mediums and natural materials. Two senses, hearing and seeing, are activated simultaneously, making new aesthetic experiences possible. With a pronounced sense of mission the artist takes possession of large spaces, drawing visitors into a dark, wired labyrinth, where they must re-orient themselves with headphones. This takes place with a presumption rare for a visual artist though, for a musician, the transmission of unique and dominant sound waves into space is a required condition. In contrast, Kubisch, as a visual artist, conserves her sound zones in the form of cables, transforming sound into a visual presentation that relates to the given space as well as achieving a kind of permanence, a quality which performed music does not share.

By inventing a sound-producing cable, Kubisch is indebted to contemporary music for she opposes the aura of uniqueness which surrounds a concert by emphasizing the possibility of reproducing sound. A remark by John Cage comes close to describing her artistic concept: "We have learned from Eastern thinking that those divine influences are in fact nothing other than the environment in which we find ourselves. A clear and calm spirit is one in which the ego does not obstruct the flow of those things which enter into us through our senses and rise up in us through our dreams. Our task in life is to take the life we are living and with it enter the flow, which is something art can help us with."[1]

This audio and visual combination serves to create, as did the Arte Povera artists, what Germano Celant termed a *prassi di fusione*, permitting flexible handling of materials and aesthetic means in order to, on the one hand, undermine cultural hierarchies and, on the other, to escape the distresses of the reality in art. Kubisch contributes to this examination through two mediums, aural and visual, and simulates tonal charms which are elevated to an enchanted idyll, exposing an often icy landscape.

Both indoors and out, Kubisch drew on recent developments in her art to create the audio works in Banff. Indoors, she developed an autonomous sculpture,

1. John Cage, quoted in Richard Kostelanetz, *John Cage* (New York: Praeger, 1970), 105.

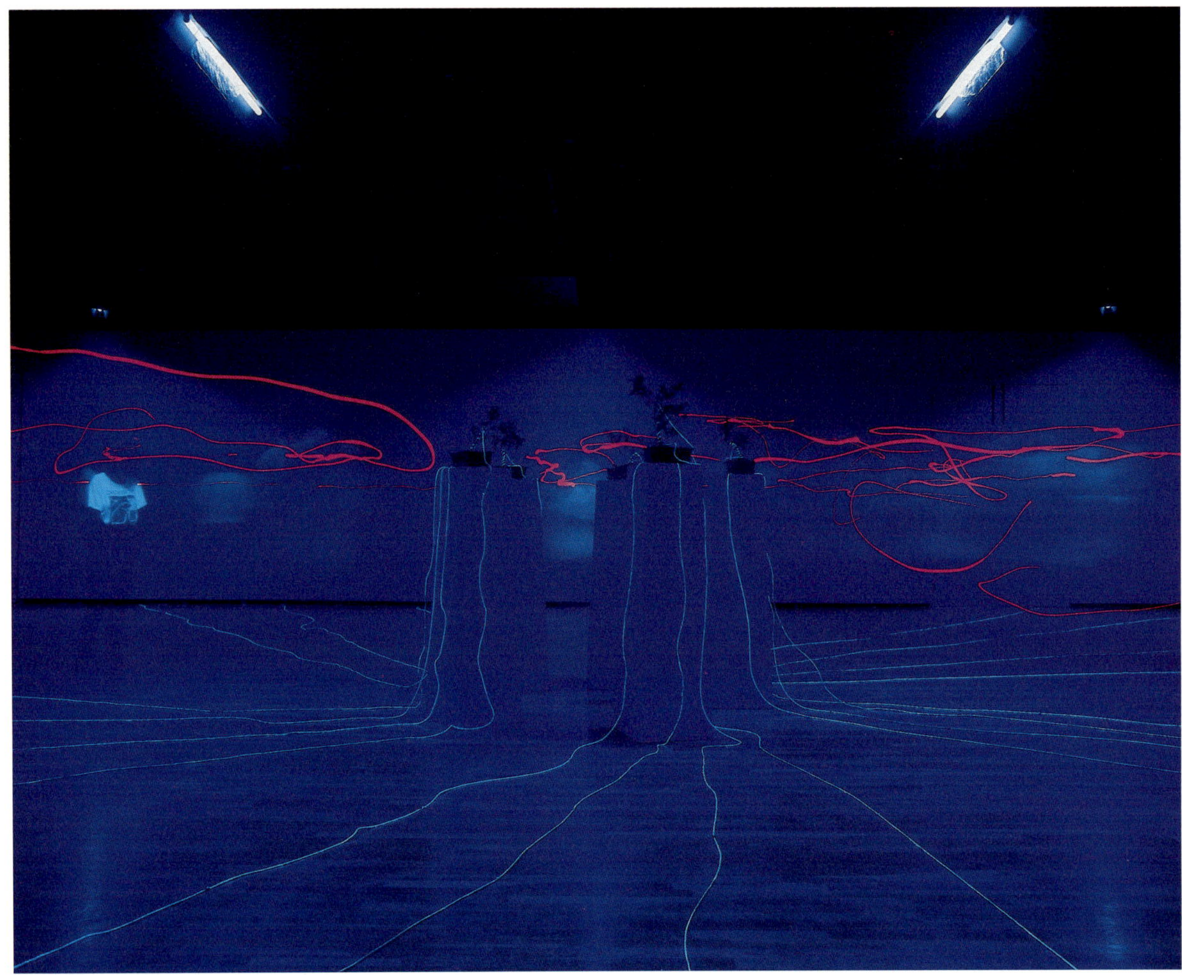

Christina Kubisch
Landscape 1989
audio installation
Photo: Douglas Curran

opposite:

Christina Kubisch
Landscape 1989
audio installation (detail)
Photo: Douglas Curran

Landscape, *with sound-carrying cables emanating physically and aurally into the black-lit gallery space. Five twisted bonsai trees, elevated as evidence of manipulated nature, form a glowing centre from which the roots appear to grow. But the fluorescent roots flowing from these ancient trees obviously are energized elsewhere, and thus the artist strikes a chord of visual contradiction. Inverted expectations provoke the viewer to consider how we understand nature in advanced technological states. Self-reflexive awareness is inevitable as the viewer is an accomplice in the creation of the piece. Wearing wireless headphones that pick up the soundwaves, the viewer moves through the space, interacting with the audiotracks emanating from each of the roots. The resulting compositions, heard only by the viewer/creator, provoke reflection on oneself as part of nature in a technological society.*

The mountain park environment of Banff, which provides a pointed context for reflection on nature, was also used by Kubisch to create an outdoor audio installation, Song for the Rockies. *Working with opposing sounds — natural and electronic — she diminished the distance between nature and technology. Her outdoor installation was meant for humans, but attracted animals who were compelled by the noise emanating from speakers placed in the hillside. Typically, high-pitched electronic sounds are used in the countryside to warn or scare off animals. Inverting the role of these electronic sounds, Kubisch lowered the pitch within the range of human hearing to create a contemplative babble approximating animal noises themselves. Like her black light installations in which the invisible is made visible, this outdoor work makes the inaudible audible. Exposing this other reality reflects the artist's perception of the potential that lies beneath the surface. Creative listening offers avenues for the exploration of technology in ways it was not intended, for as Kubisch admits, while she may hold romantic notions about technology, she also is mistrustful of it. Alternative realities provoke viewers to assess their positions in a different light, heightening awareness of context and raising the possibility of alternative interpretations not only of technology but of their environments.*

Both artist and audience are complicit in Kubisch's attempt to foster creative listening, for she starts from the premise that "listening is, in itself, an activity that must be consciously learned and developed." [2] *With the interplay of visual audio and audible visuals, Kubisch attempts to dismantle the one-way flow of music from source to listener and to engage the viewer in the production of sound, to refute the electronically-controlled "perfection" that "discourages listeners from indulging in musical activities themselves."* [3] *In her indoor work, the listener is able to compose musical sequences by choosing location and patterns of movement. Outdoors, the audience is engaged by the dynamics of man-made sounds in natural environments. Kubisch's project to stimulate awareness of aural interaction with the world creates a space for reflection on those places of time.*

Adapted from an essay by Hans Dickel, "Orte der Zeit," *Christina Kubisch, Orte der Zeit* (Munich: Kunstraum München, 1989), 7–11; translated from German by Ingrid Dinter; editorial notes by Mary Anne Moser.

2. Christina Kubisch, "About My Installations," *Sound By Artists*, eds. Dan Lander and Micah Lexier (Toronto: Art Metropole and Banff: Walter Phillips Gallery, 1990), 72.

3. Ibid., 72.

EYE OF NATURE I
November 12 to December 17, 1989

Christina Kubisch

Landscape 1989
audio/sculpture installation: 6 bonsai trees on stands, flourescent cables, 6 cassette decks, adapted headphones in black-lit room
15.1 x 21.9 m installation area
Courtesy: the artist

Song for the Rockies 1989
outdoor audio installation: adapted ultrasonic devices among rocks and trees on hillside slope
4 x 4 m installation area
Courtesy: the artist

CARROLL MOPPETT

Dreamland

DREAMLAND

David Garneau

To photograph an animal is to capture it in human discourse. Taking and viewing these photographs is the re-visioning of nature in the eye of the beholder since we cannot see animals apart from human conceptions – of them and of ourselves. Reading *Dreamland* involves our conceptual release of animals from one imprisoning textualization only to corral them into another, more personal narrative. Carroll Moppett's photo-based bookwork is a self-conscious reflection on the capture, measurement and release, not only of actual animals, but of our ideas and images of nature.

Dreamland is comprised of eight black and white photographs: a cougar watches as its paw is measured, a polar bear is loaded onto a research vessel, another has its tooth extracted and blood is taken, caribou stampede, a cast is made of a grizzly's mouth, an eagle is weighed, a cougar's teeth are displayed in a man's hand, a bear gazes toward the camera. In all but two images, a tranquillized, non-domesticated, North American animal is manipulated by partly visible or implied humans. These are not amateur photographs, they are documentations of scientific research or its facsimile.

There is something both familiar and strange about these photographs. Pictures of men and drugged animals are stock images for nature magazines. While *Dreamland's* photographs are similarly nature-oriented, they seem dislocated, their genre, purpose and even content, not entirely clear. They elicit sympathy, curiosity and anxiety, as images of stupefied animals manipulated for unspecified reasons. Moppett's photographs appear to be deliberate representations, but reading their intent is obscured by specific absences, particularly the exclusion of accompanying text that would explain the images, and the cropping of vital parts of the picture which might have established context. However, we could take these absences as entrances through which *Dreamland* can be engaged as an open work challenging the way we represent, conceptualize and use animals in dominant Western cultures.

Anyone familiar with nature magazines, particularly those of the 1960s and 1970s may recognize the inspiration for *Dreamland's* images. These journals provided a digested version of scientific exploration for everyday consumption. Aside from capturing versions of other peoples, they specialized in narratives about man's heroic struggle to save nature. This form of storytelling might be called naturalization: just as people from other societies are alien until assimilated (naturalized) into the adoptive society's master narrative, animals too are not considered beings in themselves but instead are described, defined and captured by people. Other beings seem only to exist in relation to our concepts and stories — netted by our concepts of nature.

While animal species and location vary in each nature magazine story, a unifying narrative structures the words and frames the photographs. The magazine reproductions and accompanying text tend to construct the subject to conform to the story of "man," as represented by the humane (male) scientist who cares for nature, by capturing, drugging, measuring, tagging and monitoring animals. The narrative normally associated with this genre of documentation implies that *man* momentarily harms nature for *her* own good. Accompanying texts, as those found in nature magazines, present the viewer with an authoritative description/reading, discouraging if not silencing alternate interpretations, impressing its code upon the compliant reader. Without labels, researchers become simply people, the image of the benevolent scientist fades and their actions may be interpreted as human behaviour rather than scientific research. No longer protected by the professional status imparted by captions, these men and their actions can then be interpreted through viewer's experience. The hands holding open the jaws of an anaesthetized grizzly bear seem to sign, on our behalf, unlimited power through technology. Moppett's intervention purges the images, opening them not so they might speak for themselves, but so we might make our own meanings with them.

Moppett may have chosen these older illustrations, even though the same types occur now, because they were published at a time when the gendering of science and nature was a common and seemingly unproblematic practice. Just as it is easier to detect sexism and ethnocentrism in advertisements from the sixties, so gendering, commodification and scientism are easier to read in nature photographs of twenty years ago.

Dreamland's representations of nature magazine photographs are even more disturbing than the originals due to subtle changes that occur in the artist's subversive modifications. Moppett's cropping fractures the prescribed reading. By removing portions of an image, the original compositional hierarchy is shifted: when researchers are only marginally represented – by hands, clothing, implication – the animals become the principal subject. The reading of the photographs shifts from *science acting upon,* to *animals being acted upon.* Moppett's subterfuge disrupts the benevolent, heroic, science narrative so that its effect on animals as opposed to its potency becomes the primary theme. The photographs are re-presented for re-reading (remedial reading) within a context that calls attention to the surviving animal.

In re-presenting these images, Moppett chooses not to reproduce them in their original colour. The more-real-than-real Kodachrome colour of 1960s magazine photography is displaced by black and white. Difficult to locate in time, these pictures now evoke pain, helplessness and the legacy of abuse in general. Black and white photographs, as incomplete, colourless representations, can be read as interpretations rather than copies of reality. As interpretations they suggest the presence of the eye behind the lens and our eye/I as implicated viewers. The selectivity of vision is highlighted and the resulting awareness raises questions that cannot be answered authoritatively according to prescribed meaning. Opened in this way, these images resist closure and thus the artist's intervention makes our viewing self-conscious: we catch ourselves seeing.

Moppett's reproductions also show the exaggerated Benday dots which result from enlarging – not original photographs – but magazine reproductions. Moppett's strategy is to make clear that she is not the original photographer, but that her role is that of intervener. While professional colour photographs may be perceived as windows onto a scene, Moppett's reproductions direct attention to the materiality of the photograph. Like looking through a filter, attention shifts between the distant view and the immediate surface, provoking awareness of the photographs as constructions rather than windows to reality. The original magazine photographs operate as mirrors of petrified nature, presenting subjects only as they are under surveillance. Moppett's work acts as a reminder that imaged animals are imagined animals, subjects of cultural projection.

Though Moppett uses technical plays and tropes to reveal the narratives that structure our vision of nature, her images remain embedded in human discourse. Here, as elsewhere, the making of meaning itself requires a conceptualization of animals: no imaged animal escapes the snare of human constructs. However, the colonization of physical, factual animal bodies differs from the use of animal images as symbol and metaphor. Moppett engages the difference by constructing *Dreamland* in a profoundly self-conscious manner. How can we begin to understand the meaning of events recorded in photographs without examining photographs as potentially problematic depictions of reality? It is evident that Moppett's intent is not to rescue animals from being pictured, but to have us recognize how animals are conceptualized.

Animal images are integral to the symbolism of cultures that identify themselves within nature. Cultures that symbiotically engage the environment represent animals not only as sources of food and shelter, but also as sources of meaning and identity: animal beings and human beings are expressed as intertwined realities. For those who differentiate their selves from their environment, images of animals are trophies, records of capture and colonization. Western industrial societies tend to position the environment as other, the essential not-I. Nature thereby is constructed as the mirror opposite which defines us: the eye of nature is the mirror upon which we project our animal selves — it is the eye (I) of the not-I. Nature beholds our loss.

Dreamland's animal tale is a story of loss and recovery and the expression of deeply felt pain. The record of events occurring on the bodies of animals may resonate in the bodies of those with similar experiences. This personal narrative then goes beyond specific inscriptions of science to embody the effects of the general gaze, capturing, examining, marking, releasing and monitoring the bodies of the unempowered. To be explicit, the images may resonate strongly for survivors of abuse under the hands of people inscribed as dominant.

Looking at the pictures again, as they are now re-figured, our emotions may suffuse the viewing. In sympathy we can feel the rapidly beating heart flushed with fear-induced adrenalin, the baffled, confused and coerced passivity resulting from tranquilizer darts that defraud muscles, nerves and instincts. Prostrate bodies are drugged into submission, into the probing hands of men taking their measure. Viewer's reactions are limited to kinesthetic empathy, to allowed bodily experiences in accord with what we see. The disorientation of the not-I animal echoes a human ordeal and the imaged empathy with the other becomes an owning of experience.

Dreamland, the land of dreams, is the realm where the unconscious mirrors its multiple appearances and the dreamer cannot help but play along. Carroll Moppett's *Dreamland* is a painful recovery of one's own(ed) visual sight and bodily site, a poetic effort to reclaim experience. By seizing fragments of the master('s) code, Moppett also manages to cipher her way in and out of her own inscription.

CONTESTED TERRAIN

Helga Pakasaar

Human relationships with the natural world are invariably confounding. Realizing that any depiction of nature is socially constructed, many contemporary artists are nevertheless concerned with the obscurity of nature. During this century, modernists have responded to the "new nature" of technology, preferring to botanize the urban landscape, but now, with ecological crises, the natural environment is demanding more attention. The works of Jeffrey Spalding and Ritsuko Taho selected for the exhibition *Eye of Nature II* reveal the attempts of two contemporary artists to grapple with this loaded subject by invoking the aesthetic of landscape. An imagined perception composed of what is both seen and thought, landscape is a cultural image, a social discourse. In Spalding's paintings and Taho's installation, landscape ideals from cultural traditions of the West and with Taho, also the East, are reinterpreted from an urban perspective. Inspired by sites like Banff National Park, their works also refer to mass consumption of nature through tourism and the ideology of so-called wilderness parks — government territory that is uncultivated yet highly managed and marketed. The impulse to mark a site, whether an artistic or political act, is always determined by cultural assumptions about the meaning of *land, earth* and *territory*, meanings that shift with social change as is evident in the ideological debates of current world politics. Any image of landscape then — whether verbal, visual or physical — reveals that knowledge of nature is always limited by cultural perspectives.

The acculturation of nature is addressed in this exhibition through a reframing of nature as spectacle. For Spalding this involves personalizing stereotypical images of idealized nature. Quoting from a picturesque postcard or a detail from a Romantic painting, he subverts the mediations of pictorial convention and naturalist illusion through abstraction. Ritsuko Taho also undermines the alienating effect of sightseeing by affirming an intimate, sensory experience of landscape. Her installation, *Beginning of Memory*, is apprehended initially as a scenic vista, but a pathway physically draws the viewer into the seductive spaces of this three-dimensional painting. While retaining a theatricality, the spectacle of nature in these landscape works becomes an unstable, dissolving topography, one which invokes the experiential immediacy of "wild" nature. Direct, unmediated communion with nature, however, remains an illusion, as landscape invariably implies separation and observation.

As suggested by the exhibition's title, Taho and Spalding acknowledge that the eye, whether mechanical or biological, always screens subjectivity through cultural perspective. The meditative quality of their atmospheric, "sky water" imagery also intimates Thoreau's concept of "earth's eye."[1] This impulse to link nature with human sensibilities can be considered in terms of the sublime, a moribund aesthetic that continues to gain currency. The sublime has traditionally been associated with a desire to locate *authentic* perception, a desire that persists despite, and perhaps because of, the common belief that representation is a simulation, a text that can be decoded. Spalding's and Taho's works have a formalist restraint infused with emotional disquiet, a rationalism trying to contain wreckless disorder. Sublime nature is, after all, always a tamed beast. However, unlike the absolutism of the romantic sublime which purports to face all-powerful nature directly, the idea of spiritual humility expressed by these artists is based on a skepticism about the possibility of transcendence. In an era of space travel when electronic media can produce discernible images of what was once only known as *the great beyond*, the idea of infinite space is no longer so astonishing. A longing for actual vastness inhabits the unsettled skies pervading these landscapes. This is a *conceptual sublime*[2] that acknowledges the distance between referent and sign, truth and delusion. The ideology of the sublime is inherently related to melancholy and, as Thomas Weiskel has suggested, "in its more energetic renditions the sublime is a kind of homeopathic therapy, a cure of uneasiness by means of the stronger, more concentrated — but momentary — anxiety involved in astonishment and terror."[3] Although Spalding's and Taho's wish-landscapes promise harmony, they are infiltrated with a sense of loss, a spiritual homelessness. Any nostalgic yearning for lost illusions is overpowered by the chilly air of the uninhabited, amorphous spaces. As belief in the autonomous self continues to disintegrate, any expression of awe is necessarily a cautionary, qualified gesture.

Light has traditionally been the primary vehicle for evoking the sublime and both artists exploit its metaphoric power as an illuminating and blinding force that artic-

1. Thoreau describes Walden Pond as a transcendental ideal: "It is earth's eye; looking into which the beholder measures the depth of his own nature...a perfect forest mirror....Sky water." Quoted in Barbara Novak, *Nature and Culture: American Landscape and Painting, 1825–1875* (New York: Oxford University Press, l980), 41.

2. Gregory Galligan, "Rescripting the Sublime," *Art International* 7 (Summer 1989), 56–9. As with other landscape aesthetics like the pastoral and picturesque, the notion of the sublime is continually being revamped, most recently with Jean-Francois Lyotard's treatise on the "postmodern sublime" and Jacques Derrida's notion of the "transcendental."

3. Thomas Weiskel, *The Romantic Sublime: Studies in the Structure and Psychology of Transcendence* (Baltimore and London: John Hopkins University Press, 1976), 6.

Jeffery Spalding
Event 1989
oil on canvas
Photo: Douglas Curran

ulates as well as makes things disappear. Spalding emulates techniques for render-ing natural light from the history of Western landscape painting, particularly the inner glow effect and mirror-like surfaces typical of American Luminism. Diaphanous light accentuates reflection, and as with the shimmering effect of wax glazing, substance is distinguished from the immaterial through subtle shifts in tone. Having a mood of imminent bad weather, Spalding's landscapes retain dark secrets teased by the disclosures of light. Similarly, Taho's subterranean space is animated by beams of light. The illumination of this tableau is overtly theatrical and contrived, yet its sources seem natural — the sun, moon, stars, phosphorus. In a rather painterly manner, Taho uses light to fracture surfaces and create space: blue walls enclosing a pool of water become skies punctuated by shadows, windows of light, and fields of reflected rippling water. It is the immateriality of light that is stressed in these depictions of nature's moments of dissolve, making its ability to both magnify and diffuse the particular a palpable metaphor for subjectivity.

In response to the wilderness setting of Banff, the artists interiorize and domesti-cate landscape into constricted, contained spaces. The chaotic forces of nature are controlled, distilled and abstracted. Specifics of place are reduced to the basic ele-ments of earth, air and water and rendered as abstract fields of light and colour. Less emphatic than earthwork interventions, eco-art polemics or the neo-romantic nostalgia of many contemporary landscape paintings, the works of Spalding and Taho approach nature with a subdued skepticism. Fueled by a yearning for the immediacy of direct contact, even reconciliation, with the natural world, they chart the uncertain boundaries between civilization and wilderness.

Jeffrey Spalding's sensibility is informed by this tension between control and dis-order, evident in recent as well as earlier work. His explorations into the struc-tural language of video processes in the early seventies led to systemic painting. The *Black Paintings* (1973-75), a series of square canvasses heavily layered with colours until the surface appears black, are an ironic comment on the ostensible inertness of monochromes. Since then, Spalding's paintings have become increas-ingly representational, yet he is still involved with undermining the structures of a

Jeffery Spalding
Dark Union 1988
oil and wax on board
Photo: Douglas Curran

given system through a deliberate and overdetermined process of destabilization. In recent years, as in the work included in *Eye of Nature II*, Spalding has conflated the restrictive principles of abstraction with naturalist illusion. More concerned with expressing the desire to find meaning rather than narrative meaning alone, his stance remains skeptical, an ironic negation of subjectivity. Always interested in predetermined systems, he works primarily from images found in art history publications, post cards and advertising. Spalding proposes an uneasy truce with these idealized views of nature typical of popularized landscape. His paintings, although emotive, are conflicted denials of the desire to be moved by sentiment. While they are formalist and analytical, an agitated tension underlies the measured pattern of brushstrokes. Too wary to be nostalgic, their lyrical moments are only a temporary avoidance of disillusion. Spalding's minimal foregrounds and shallow spaces leave no solid ground for projecting human presence. Unable to rest beyond surface and texture, the disembodied viewer becomes distanced and contemplative.

In *Dark Union* (1986), Spalding re-presents a generic image of awe-inspiring natural splendour, Niagara Falls, as a site of existential dread, thwarting its grandeur. A diptych of mirror images, this panorama is a telescopic view of a dark abyss exuding menacing vapours, introspective apparitions. Similarly brooding and nocturnal, the luminous waterfall of *Dark Source: Threshold* (1987) descends from darkness into deeper darkness. These are places for lucid dreams. Still identifiable as natural sites, in his more recent works such as *Evolve* (1988) based on a Turner painting of a dust storm, abstract space is only vaguely suggestive of natural phenomena. Amorphous forms are charged with an ethereal glow coming from an unknown source, an effect that is repeated in *Event* (1989). Inspired by a newspaper photograph, *Event* emits a sinister energy with its red and purple clouds like fiery noxious fumes of chemical, perhaps even atomic, pollution. Spalding's images have increasingly focussed on parts of sky, "the soul of all scenery" according to the Luminists. Their vertical format and telescopic perspective emphasize the intensity of Spalding's controlled expressionism. Details cropped from a larger picture, these fragments are seemingly introspective yet they invoke the idea of vastness, creating the tension of an "intimate immensity."[4]

Ritsuko Taho also expresses the micro/macro inversions of the natural world through distortions of scale. Although often monumental in size, her works lack the authority and closure of monoliths. They are often diffuse and disarrayed, as if caught in a state of transformation. Most of her site-specific installations and sculptures are concerned with the persistence of natural forces, particularly in relation to urban life. Addressing the interaction of human and natural environments, Taho's works constructed from industrial and organic materials are subjected to natural and social processes, whether outdoors or in a gallery. For instance, a process work that she developed in the early eighties involved burning rice and straw, the ashes of which became an indoor piece that eventually took on another life as an earthwork at a river site. *Forbidden Building* (1988), a twenty-four-foot-high cage attached to the side of a building, was continually changing as the leaves it contained decomposed and new ones were added by the artist as well as the local community. The unrefined look of Taho's organic constructions mirrors the instability of natural forces.

In *Beginning of Memory*, an installation commissioned for this exhibition, Taho asserts the significance of the processes of nature, especially as experienced by the human body. The strong dynamics of this piece — rigid and fluid, enclosed and vast, serene and emotional — allude to the creative and destructive forces of nature. Respecting the integrity of materials, Taho allows for change. Temporary itself, this environment is in a state of flux determined by natural processes; moving water erodes the ochre forms, organic growths proliferate and the topography evolves with evaporation. The observer's journey provides a more immediate experience of process and temporality. An abstracted landscape rich in associations, this work exudes a meditative calm that is initially reminiscent of a Japanese garden or rice field, and then, as one moves through the environment, its details recall a more ambiguous, surreal place. The rigidity of its architectonic shape, echoed in the rectilinear pathway, is contrasted with the chaos of a room-sized

4. Gaston Bachelard, *The Poetics of Space* (New York: Beacon Press, 1964), 184.

Ritsuko Taho
Beginning of Memory 1989
mixed media installation
Photo: Douglas Curran

opposite:

Ritsuko Taho
Beginning of Memory 1989
mixed media installation (detail)
Photo: Douglas Curran

Paint Pots
ochre beds in Kootenay National Park,
British Columbia
Photo: Alan Michelson

5. Susan Stewart, *On Longing: Narratives of the Miniature, the Gigantic, the Souvenir, the Collection* (Baltimore and London: John Hopkins University Press, 1984), 70, 74.

pool activated by the effects of moving water from punctured hoses. Like the site that inspired this work — ochre beds fed by springs in Kootenay National Park — the subtle, ochre tones of the clay covering the plastic floor of the pool and the stained branches floating in the water are continually moving. The pool also alludes to primordial matter as well as the effluent remains of an abandoned industrial site. As one travels through this environment — an eery topography punctuated by the sound of sputtering liquid — the experience acquires more visceral qualities — like being inside a human body, a primal space, at the *beginning of memory*. Clay, hoses and branches take on associations of skin, veins and limbs. Taho's sensibility is akin to the Japanese concept of *haragei*, a philosophy of communication that understands nature as based in the human body (*hara*, the stomach), which proposes a subliminal contact with nature. While Spalding considers nature from a more analytical distance, Taho's landscape is subjectified through bodily experience. Yet, as with Spalding's work, the observer retreats from sensual immediacy to contemplate the ideal again.

While disturbing the illusion of spectacle, the works of Taho and Spalding confirm the theatrical and sensual aspects of nature. Like the idea of *sky water*, these ambiguous spaces conflate interior and exterior worlds. In an attempt to reduce the irreducible, landscape requires a contradictory perception. As Susan Stewart has described: "Whereas the miniature represents closure, interiority, the domestic, and the overly cultural,...a mental world of proportion, control and balance,...the gigantic represents infinity, exteriority, the public, and the overly natural....a physical world of disorder and disproportion."[5] Human interaction with the natural world, then, can be understood as inherently paradoxical. For many contemporary artists, the subject of nature provides a temporary ground for confirming the human by considering what lies beyond it. Whether revising conventional views of landscape, like Spalding, or creating an imaginary site through personal language, like Taho, it is precisely the intractability of their subject that is relevant, especially in light of modern society's perilous alienation from nature.

Jeffrey Spalding

Dark Union 1986
oil and wax on board
2 panels, each 93 x 203 cm
Courtesy: Waddington and Shiell Galleries

Dark Source: Threshold 1987
oil on canvas
244 x 168 cm
Collection: Eija Iris and Cecil Wishart

Ascending 1988
oil on canvas
267 x 170 cm
Courtesy: Waddington and Shiell Galleries

Evolve 1988
oil on canvas
170 x 340 cm
Courtesy: Waddington and Shiell Galleries

Event 1989
oil on canvas
244 x 168 cm
Courtesy: Diane Farris Gallery

Range 1989
pastel on paper
127.5 x 278 cm
Courtesy: Waddington and Shiell Galleries

Ritsuko Taho

Beginning of Memory 1989
wood, paint, rubber, clay, ochre, water, branches,
plastic hose, pump
10.5 x 11.7 m installation area
Courtesy: the artist

RODNEY GRAHAM

Flanders Trees

OAK, KAGGEVINNE. 1989.

OAK, MELLAAR. 1989.

LINDEN, RONSE. 1989

WILLOW, MULLEM. 1989.

LINDEN, HUNDELGEM. 1989.

SIGHTING THE SINGLE TREE
SIGHTING THE NEW FOUND LAND

Matthew Teitelbaum

"There is no centre any longer,
and the sacred tree is dead."
Black Elk, prophet of the Oglala Sioux, in 1931[1]

For many Canadians, the single tree strikes a particularly nationalistic image. It has come to stand for landscape as a singular genre of painting, as much a symbol of untamed and virtuous nature as can be found. And yet, although Biblical and European antecedents for the imaging of the single tree had long been a cornerstone of nineteenth-century cultured learning, it was not until the 1920s, and the frequent public exhibition of their pictures, that the Group of Seven and Tom Thomson popularized the image of the lone pine tree for the Canadian public. In the popular imagination and the mythos of a new Dominion, the twisting, windswept single tree, with its art nouveau and German romantic inspirations, came to symbolize a pioneering spirit crystallizing at the edge of an unknown space.

The Group's nationalist mythology was rooted in the image of the pioneer as explorer and adventurer, and traditional narratives of the Group of Seven's enterprise have celebrated a movement which "shows that when the soul of man and the soul of his people and the environment meet, the creative genius of a race bursts into flames."[2] Their trips from British Columbia to Newfoundland may be seen as a search for "the 'essence' of Canada."[3] In such a reading, the single tree marked a cherished signpost along a journey or a promised site of arrival — the great panoramic viewpoint, the potential homestead, the site of abundance. As markers of site and place, however, the single tree imaged by the Group of Seven also tied the landscape irrevocably to questions of possession and territorialization. A reading of the image of the single tree, particularly in relation to the work of contemporary artists who now work with nature-based images, may be linked to historical narratives of cultural dominance grounded in the material world of land ownership. The conflicted relationship between cultural privilege and the histories of marginalized populations which has been interrogated by a number of contemporary Canadian artists — Bill Reid, Edward Poitras, Judith Doyle, Robert Fones and Rodney Graham among them — is tied specifically to the question of how contested land ownership issues might alter the way we look at landscape in Canada. While drawing upon issues of territorialization, these artists have used images and representations from the natural world, in some cases the single tree itself, to symbolize new economic and cultural

1. Quoted in Joan Vastokas, "The Shamanistic Tree of Life," *artscanada* (December 1973/January 1974), 125.

2. Fred B. Housser, *A Canadian Art Movement* (Toronto: Macmillan, 1926; reprint, 1974), 215.

3. Ibid., 135.

Tom Thomson
The West Wind 1917
oil on canvas
Collection: Art Gallery of Ontario
Gift of the Canadian Club of Toronto, 1926
Photo: Art Gallery of Ontario

4. Lawren Harris, "The Group of Seven in Canadian History," *Canadian Historical Association: Report of the Annual Meeting held at Victoria and Vancouver June 16–19, 1948* (Toronto: Canadian Historical Association, 1948), 28.

5. Ibid., 36.

orders. With reference to the founding, traditional work of the Group of Seven, it is thus possible to juxtapose the ideology of colonialism with its aftermath, the moment of the postcolonial, and to link territorialization to new configurations of national and international populations.

I

In the first decades of this century, the self-generating mythology of the Group of Seven highlighted the tree as a touchstone for that experience of nature which evoked feelings of belonging and attachment to new territory. Lawren Harris, a founding member of the Group, wrote of the pioneering experience as elemental:

> The first task of our forefathers in this new land was altogether a pioneering one; clearing the wilderness, establishing settlements, making roads to connect one place with the next, organizing the settlements and cultivated areas into workable communities, and later forming all sections of the country into the semblance of a nation.[4]

Harris tied the pioneer's quest to the artist's search. For him, as for other members of the Group, the painter's exploration of new regions paralleled the assertion of a national spirit. Exploration grounded a "deep and vital experience of [a] total environment"[5] and evoked that sense of communal attachment which was necessary for any claims to nationhood. Harris' conviction that the "spirit of the land" bound disparate peoples together reflected both the optimism of Wilfrid Laurier's 1904 prime ministerial pronouncement that "the twentieth century shall be filled by Canada," and the immigration policies of the Liberal government in the years from 1896 onwards – policies which actively solicited emigration from central and eastern Europe with the hope of populating the open and "uncultivated" western Canadian grain belt. Tracts of viable farm land were offered in solicitation campaigns which promised both bountiful harvests and rewarding adventure. In a manner that mirrored the widespread selling of the Canadian wilderness in tourist literature of the late nineteenth century, western Canada's open spaces were promoted among prospective settlers as the true frontier. In the mythos of the new Dominion, both settler and tourist ventured into a space of limitless amplitude and possibility.

The Group of Seven shared such belief in the mutability of experience and nation-hood. When A.Y. Jackson introduced the second Group of Seven exhibition at the Art Gallery of Toronto in 1920, his text paralleled the nation-building proclamations of turn of the century governments. Declaring, "These are still pioneer days for artists, and after the fashion of pioneers we believe wholeheartedly in the land,"[6] Jackson built upon a land-based nationalist rhetoric long in place.[7] The Group tied an experience of being in the landscape to a spiritual renewal, and such renewal to a reformulation of culture. Open space represented freedom, and freedom allowed the assertion of a national character. It was a purifying element in consciousness. Indeed, for the Group, spiritual freedom was evoked through the very presumption of a new world, the open space beyond the horizon. To get beyond what was known, to get "out there" in the unexplored countryside, was to move beyond the established frontier into a new identity rooted in exploration. Thus, Lawren Harris could write:

> From the cities, towns and countrysides, to the far reaches of the northern ice-fields it was an even clearer and deeply moving experience of oneness with the spirit of the whole land. It was this spirit which dictated, guided and instructed us how the land should be painted. To us there was also the strange brooding sense of another nature fostering a *new race and a new age* [my italics].[8]

And thus could the Group mirror the claims of spokesmen for the new Dominion such as Clifford Sifton, the Minister of the Interior in Laurier's cabinet, who declared in an effort to encourage immigration to the Canadian West in the early 1900s: "One of the principal ideas western men have is that it is right to take anything in sight provided nobody is ahead of them."[9] This notion of the frontier marking a space beyond which individuals would thrive was implicitly linked to a broadly shared belief that diverse immigrant groups could be assimilated into the Canadian culture through the favourable influence of Anglo-Saxon tradition. While Sifton welcomed increased immigration from both central and eastern European countries with the famous phrase: "I think a stalwart peasant in a sheep-skin coat, born on the soil, whose forefathers have been farmers for ten generations, with a stout wife and a half-dozen children, is good quality,"[10] his invitation was set within a nationalist framework refracted over and over again, symp-

6. Quoted in A.Y. Jackson, *A Painter's Country* (Toronto: Clarke, Irwin and Company Limited, 1976), 65.

7. This nationalist rhetoric recently had been underlined through the fervour for victory during the First World War.

8. Harris, 36–7.

9. Quoted in Desmond Morton, *A Short History of Canada* (Edmonton: Hurtig Publishers, 1983), 122.

10. Quoted in Richard Clippingdale, *Laurier: His Life and World* (Toronto: McGraw Hill, 1979), 75.

tomatically in a *Winnipeg Free Press* editorial of July 8th, 1898: "Canada is Anglo-Saxon and will remain Anglo-Saxon. Foreigners may come in their thousands, and they, too, if not in the first, then in the second generation, will also be Anglo-Saxon."[11]

The Group of Seven's imaged nature held a central place within such paradigms of race and nationhood. Writing in 1958, Canadian literary theorist Northrop Frye noted the Group's romantic and subjective tendencies in comments about the Confederation poets of the mid-nineteenth century who

> were at best when confronting nature in solitude, in moods of nostalgia, reverie, observation, or extrasensory awareness. Their sensibility is emotional in origin, and they attain conceptual precision by emotional precision....This subjective and lyrical sensibility, sharp and clear in its emotional foreground but inclined to get vague around the conceptual fringes, is deeply rooted in the Canadian tradition. Most of its characteristics appear in the Group of Seven painters, in Tom Thomson and Emily Carr, with their odd mixture of art nouveau and cosmic consciousness.[12]

Within iconographic categories of landscape representation, the Group's image of the single tree, particularly, played upon the drama of solitude and evoked the artists' deeply felt connection to environment. As a signifier of man "out there" in nature, the tree was a point of entry to the landscape. It grounded that sensation which Harris called the "moving experience of oneness with the spirit of the whole land."[13] The many works by Tom Thomson and the Group which image an isolated tree twisting in a ravaging storm are layered to elicit empathy in the viewer through a signification of mortal man, alone and heroic. The single tree represents, in one sense, survival at the edge of the frontier. It underlines, in Arthur Lismer's words, both a sympathy with "the lakes, trees, and all the elements of beauty in the Canadian background,"[14] and, more directly, "the spirit of Canada made manifest in a picture."[15] This spirit, in the terms set by the Group, was one of struggle, endurance, and finally, triumph in the midst of a rugged and hostile nature.[16]

Yet, in another sense, the tree marked more than the individual's immediate and specific place; it also implied a tie to the country as a whole — literally beyond the horizon, figuratively beyond the frontier of civilization. With few exceptions, the Group of

11. Quoted in Marilyn Barber, "Introduction," to J.S. Wordsworth, *Strangers Within Our Gates* (Toronto: University of Toronto Press, 1972), xvi.

12. Northrop Frye, "Poetry," *The Arts in Canada: A Stock-Taking at Mid-Century*, ed. Malcolm Ross (Toronto: Macmillan, 1958), 84.

13. Harris, 36–37.

14. This was a comment about Tom Thomson's epic *The West Wind* in Arthur Lismer, *Canadian Picture Study* (Toronto: The Art Gallery of Toronto, 1940), 19. I am grateful for this and a number of subsequent references to Carolyn McHardy, "The West Wind" (Unpublished Master's Thesis, Queen's University, Kingston, 1977).

15. This was also a comment on *The West Wind* which Lismer made in his article "The West Wind," *The McMaster Monthly* 43 (January 1935), 163.

16. Harris wrote emphatically about the artist's struggle to wrest images from the landscape. Recalling the experience of watching Tom Thomson paint in a storm, Harris wrote: "Here was symbolized, it came to me, the function of the artist in life: he must accept a deep singleness of purpose, the manifestations of life in man and in nature, and transform them into controlled and ordered and vital expressions of meaning" (33). Harris underlines Thomson's connection to the ravaged subjects of his paintings.

Seven's imaged tree stands isolated in foreground space before a panoramic sweep of the landscape.[17] Its presence inflects upon the landscape about it, issuing a declaration of unity through identification with territory. Indeed, it stands as a symbol of the individual most particularly in relation to the panorama it proclaims as its own.

A reading of the tree, as attachment through territory, raises questions. By whom, and for what cause, are claims established upon territory? The Group's characterizations of landscape implied a prosperity based upon that degree of civilization which would develop within an unknown space. To picture that space or, quite literally to make pictures out of it, was to possess it in some manner; in Harris' words, it was to create "controlled and ordered and vital expressions of meaning."[18] And yet, to underline a point, if the landscape was to be seen as capable of transforming character and purifying consciousness, it had to develop or make something new within a newly discovered space. Such transformation was predicated on a space described as unrecorded, a space as yet unordered, for it was in that space that spirit was born out of a new social order. There is a link between a belief in new vision and discovery, and a social order that encouraged, yet controlled, increased immigration quotas. Immigration was solicited, after all, in the belief that a new, resolutely Canadian identity would proclaim itself beyond the frontier.

The presumption of transformation and development that was inherent in such a vision of Canada reinforced well established representations of an emerging nation. Canadian critic Geoff Miles has written of nineteenth-century landscape representations as expressing a colonial sense

> of the empty land slowly unfolding itself, and revealing in its folds,
> on an imaginary level, "its desire" to be filled with the desire of
> Western civilization.[19]

Extending such a reading would be to see the single tree not merely as a manifestation of man's presence in the landscape but as mapper as well, the surveyor in a long and insistent procession of "explorers." The very phrase, "emerging nation," implies an ideology of newness, tied to material achievement, as an invitation to progress.

17. The relation of an identifiable marker within the landscape, to the landscape as a whole, is one subject of much American painting of the nineteenth century. Barbara Novak writes of man-made landscape markers in "Man's Traces: Axe, Train, Figure," *Nature and Culture* (New York: Oxford University Press, 1980), 157–200.

18. Harris, 33.

19. Geoff Miles, "Topoi," *Shifting Fields: Images of Colonialism and the Look of the Postcolonial*, eds. Jennifer Oille and Geoff Miles (Toronto: Coach House Press, 1989), 13. In this important essay Miles looks at the relation between nineteenth-century artists and the patronage of class and business interests. Of particular interest to him are the images commissioned by the Canadian Pacific Railway in the 1880s – images which underline "the CPR's history of patronage and direct commissioning of photographers and painters as a way of increasing its revenues by producing 'tourism' on the one hand and 'land sale' on the other" (25).

The individual brings desire to the edge of the frontier — indeed, beyond the frontier — and evokes change through the creation of a civilized and efficient order.

II

A colonialist claim to presentness — to discovering and claiming new territory, and creating it in one's own image — by necessity obscures prior settlements. In a manner which reflects much anthropological writing of their time and ours, the Group of Seven assigned to Canada's native populations, its first peoples, the attributes of a heroic past and much-changed present. Imaging of native life was filled with lament. In 1913, for example, Lawren Harris heralded the Toronto painter Edmund Morris as one who "records the transition of the *disappearing* Indian," and prophesized that "in years to come the Western work of Morris will stand for much in our memories of the *vanished red man.*"[20] Disappearing, vanished — these are loaded words with specific meanings. They are words written in the past tense, setting the reader in a distanced relation to the subject. Writing in 1958, A.Y. Jackson recalled a 1926 trip to the Skeena River in British Columbia with anthropologist and folklorist Marius Barbeau and fellow painter Edwin Holgate:

> When we were in the area they were no longer being made, but the few remaining totem poles kept alive the memory of days when the tribes were numerous and powerful....The Indians of the West Coast *were* a remarkably creative people. Their arts, Barbeau believes, kept twenty per cent of the people occupied. But the big powerful tribes, Tsimsyans, Tlingits and Haidas, have dwindled to a mere shadow *of their former greatness.* They produce little to-day in the way of art [my italics].[21]

Native peoples were: noble, proud, authentic. Native peoples are: defeated, directionless, exotic shadows of their former selves.

In his important anthropological critique, American cultural historian James Clifford has argued that it is just such a heroicism of past native populations that maintains unequal relations of power in the present. To assign to a people a glorious past, to idealize ethics and pride, is to deny a presentness of capability and achievement. In *The Predicament of Culture*, published in 1988, Clifford develops his thesis in detail,

20. Lawren Harris, "The Canadian Art Club," *The Yearbook of Canadian Art: 1913* (London and Toronto: J.M. Dent and Sons, 1913), 215.

21. Jackson, 109, 111. In a later passage, Jackson writes of the native populations with almost hallucinogenic nostalgia. "Paddling is now a lost art; probably the husky dog will disappear, and the caribou, along with the teepee and the igloo; and the Eskimos and the Indians will wear the same store clothes as everyone else. Most of the picturesqueness had departed before the artists came into contact with it and now that many of the younger artists have gone abstract, there is little possibility that this way of life will ever be recorded" (146).

highlighting the contemporary experience of numerous so-called "primitive" cultures, whose societal and tribal lineage has been continually characterized as fetishistic and exclusionary. It is the definition of populations, of groups, of communities, that lies at the heart of Clifford's critique, and he grounds it in that moment of crisis when

> marginal peoples come into a historical or ethnographic space that has been defined by the Western imagination. "Entering the modern world," their distinct histories quickly vanish. Swept up in a destiny dominated by the capitalist West and by various technologically advanced socialisms, these suddenly "backward" peoples no longer invent local futures. What is different about them remains tied to traditional pasts, inherited structures that either resist or yield to the new but cannot produce it.[22]

In his review of the 1985 Museum of Modern Art's *Primitivism in 20th Century Art*, Clifford questioned an exhibition in which the art forms of aboriginal cultures were categorized as traditional, ascribed importance through "affinity" with Western models, and chosen with an eye on the imprimateur of age, even when Western art forms in the exhibition were the products of contemporary artists. In part, Clifford questioned the implicit denial which lay at the heart of the exhibition, namely that native artists cannot produce objects in this time and place, cannot create meaning out of their present circumstance, and cannot be seen *in the process* of making their own history. Clifford's critique was aimed at the dubious assumptions framing the exhibition. In the summer of 1989, twelve Haida paddlers delivering a war canoe carved by Haida artist Bill Reid to the Museum of Man in Paris, were greeted at points along their route by disappointed crowds who "thought they would have feather headdresses" and grumbled "These guys look modern."[23]

Bill Reid did not face such difficulties from those outside his culture in 1978 when his carved totem was raised in front of the Band Council building at Skidegate, on the Queen Charlotte Islands in British Columbia. The site of action was, after all, "out there," far removed from the metropolis. *Within his culture,* the raising of the totem was resonant with meaning. It was, on one hand, a sacred tree-form, a site marking the "Centre of the World," "the cosmic axis," and the "Tree of Life."[24]

22. James Clifford, "Introduction: The Pure Products Go Crazy," *The Predicament of Culture* (Cambridge: Harvard University Press, 1988), 5.

23. Rod Mickleburgh, "Haida Canoe Trip Up Seine Native Artist's Fantasy Come True," *The Globe and Mail*, 30 September 1989, C11.

24. Vastokas writes "Basic to most religious and ideological systems and standing at the heart of shamanistic ideology and iconography, is a conception of a sacred tree, standing at the very midpoint of the earth. This World Tree, moreover, is interchangeable with the idea of a post, pillar or axis positioned at the centre of the Universe, so that the world tree is also a cosmic axis" (126).

Village of Skidegate 1857
black and white photograph
Collection: British Columbia Archives and Record
Service (HP33784)
Photo: Anonymous

Its erection was a symbolic linking between the material and spiritual worlds, between the earth and sky.[25] On the other, it marked a site of possession for a tribe who cite the pole as a materialization of identity.

The pole inscribed an ancestral history back onto a space of cultural unravelling. Skidegate was Reid's mother's village, the place she had left in a search for the metropolis. The act of raising the pole was an act to reclaim a space for Reid's belief in a living Haida culture, to inscribe that space with its own history of pride, distinctiveness, and Indian ways of thinking. On another level, Reid asserted contemporaneity. Like Haida carver Robert Davidson who made a community pole for the Indians of neighbouring Masset in 1969, Reid eschewed reference to family traditions and the long-assumed heraldic functions of totem signs. He replaced stories of family lineage in his pole with a generalized narrative that, as Reid biographer Doris Shadbolt has noted, "was prior to, though certainly not inconsistent with, their specific mythic meanings."[26] Its erection, at least metaphorically, denied a Western reading of native culture tied simply to values of the past, to ethics of family (or tribe), to easily read clan divisions. Reid's assertion, that he carved the pole as a "memorial to the Haida of the past, not a drive to turn the clock back,"[27] suggests a broader meaning for his symbols, an Indian way of constructing images of the world. He used the totem to proclaim that imaged nature could link Indian populations, both rural and urban, to one part of their identity. In defense of native land claims to park land on the Moresby Islands in northern British Columbia, Reid noted:

> The Haidas have...been in exile, ironically more so than those who displaced them. Once all of Haida Gwaii was theirs. [Now the Haida of Skidegate and Masset] live within...narrow confines, emerging to go fishing, to visit the cities of the mainland, but hardly ever venturing back to their ancestral sites. Well that's all changed now, and the first tentative probes are now reaching out to reestablish ties with the old territories and, in places like South Moresby, to find links with the past.[28]

For Reid, art generally, and the totem, the single tree, specifically, linked a population to a new history which altered its view of territory and connectedness to that territory.

25. Ibid., 144. Vastokas adds: "In fact, the erection of a totem-pole or dwelling on the Northwest Coast constituted, as among the Maya, a symbolic reenactment of world creation...In other words, the familiar totem-pole is at once the Centre of the World, the Axis upon which the universe turns, a Tree of Life, and finally, a symbolic vehicle of communication between earth and sky."

26. Doris Shadbolt, *Bill Reid* (Vancouver: Douglas & McIntyre, 1986), 130.

27. Ibid., 172.

28. Ibid., 177–8.

In her film, *Neguaguon — Lac La Croix* (1988), Toronto artist Judith Doyle tied the Ojibway of Lac La Croix Ojibway Reserve to the wilderness lakes of Quetico Provincial Park. In her activist argument against the federal government's ban on the guiding of tourists through Quetico Provincial Park by motorboat, Doyle linked the contemporary traverse through the park with the long-established traditional activities of the Ojibway. In arguing for a continuity of place, the film highlighted leisure activity and livelihood such as the dish game, the pow wow, and the harvesting of wild rice. At the same time, contemporary leisure activities, whether the performances of country bands, or teenagers watching videos and playing pool, were cited in parallel to establish continuity as presence, not as adherence to the solely traditional pantomimes and performances of ancient rites. Contemporaneity was cited as an argument for historical presence, for recognition of rights, and not their negation. In Doyle's construct, hybrid activity inscribes itself on place, an activity both contemporary and traditional. Continuity does not assume a simple sameness. "The land out there is like a book," she remarked after completing the film, "Ojibway is not a written language. Every story begins with the name of a place, a rock or an island, and the stories are remembered by travelling to the spots and remembering the stories. It's through the geography that you remember the history. And that's the fundamental reason that the traditional culture and the land can't be separated from each other."[29]

To argue for control over the land, on behalf of a people, presupposes a clear definition of how *the people* are constituted, and what link they maintain with the contested land. Territorial claims are linked to place, land and history. In the past fifty years, numerous Indian tribes in North America have brought literally thousands of land claims and sovereignty and jurisdictional test cases against various governments. In almost all cases, ownership of defined land tracts, or access to them through recognized rights, is being contested. The land's resources are invariably at issue, either directly, as logging corridors are contested and industrial and urban centres fought over, or indirectly, as park land is maintained as government controlled wilderness tracts. In this sense land claims are about capital and are the means to generate economic security. In another sense, claims are also about his-

29. Quoted in Cameron Bailey, "Doyle's Art Gathers Political Influence," *NOW* (Toronto), 8 September 1988.

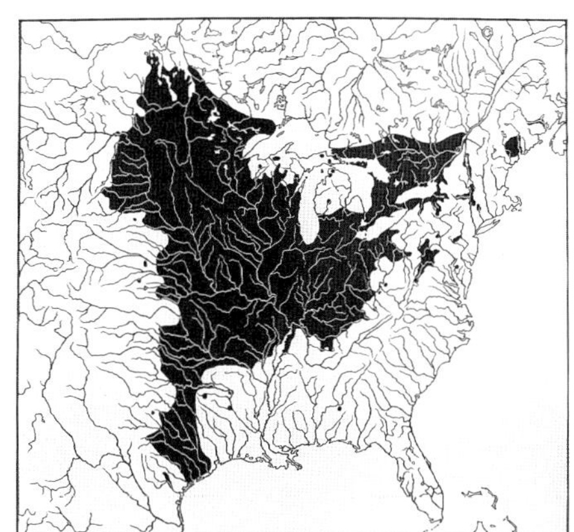

Robert Fones
Natural Range of Bur Oak 1984
woodblock print on Masa paper
Courtesy: Carmen Lamanna Gallery/Robert Fones

torical continuity, lineage, the endurance of lifestyles and customs. A legal claim to land rests upon proof of continued tribal existence and connectedness to place.

Native people's tie to the land, and their material claims to that tie, raise radical implications. Clearly, successful land claim settlements lead to a fundamental redistribution of wealth and historical privilege. New historical narratives are formed which explicitly question references to those traditional demographic categories that order, classify and define populations. In a radical extension of land claim settlements, the natural symbols used to invoke this order — the single tree, for example — are forever changed, extended that is, in their multiple readings. In his series of monumental woodblock prints, *Range Maps of Individual Tree Species* (1984), Toronto artist Robert Fones represents the growing range of various trees without regard for political boundaries. His bur oak, Canada plum and shagbark hickory traverse the Canada/United States boundary as they would prior to European contact. Cities, roads, political boundaries of all types are eliminated, not in some pre-Edenic fantasy, but as a statement about the false constraining apparatus of the nation-state and the mechanisms which ground its claim to power. Fones uses the tree to counter classification systems. His trees may be read as surrogates for native populations.

How then to make the tree into, and use the tree as, a new physical construction? How to manifest it at the centre of a world?

In a series of works which constituted the exhibition *Indian Territory*, Edward Poitras asserted a native belief. Within a museum setting layered with value systems established by the norms of Western culture, he asked for acceptance of a new consciousness. The works questioned the dominant hierarchies of a European economic order that places the individual above community. The works included among others: *White Blanket* (1988), a materialization of a ravaged 1874 treaty (which established reserves in both Saskatchewan and Southern Manitoba), ripped open with the names of the Indian signatories cut from the historical moment; *Small Matters* (1985/88), miniaturized nail and wire corrals which memorialized Indian tribes driven to extinction in the late nineteenth century; and *Internal Recall* (1985-88), a theatrical placement of seven life-

Edward Poitras
Rock Hearts 1988
installation (detail)
Courtesy: Mendel Art Gallery
Photo: A.K. Photos, Saskatoon

30. Hyemeyohsts Storm quoted in Vastokas, 140.

31. Quoted in Roger Malbert et al., *The Tree of Life: New Images of an Ancient Symbol* (London: South Bank Centre, 1989), 67.

size Indian figures, suppliant and bound, their bodies numbered for identification. In each of the works, experience was asserted as a continuum, as history. Poitras countered the rationalizations of official histories, the proclamations of nineteenth-century United States General William Sheridan, for example, who linked the near extinction of the buffalo to native overkill, to the traditions of aboriginal peoples. Poitras highlighted, as a cultural ceremony of renewal and as an emblem of moral victory, the Plains Indian Sun Dance, forbidden by Canadian law for 66 years following the implementation of the Indian Act in 1885. At its centre, a centre Poitras cherished and proclaimed, stood a single tree. This "flowering tree" stood at the true centre of a circle, and actualized the universe and signified "an entire people as a whole."[30] The great Sioux leader, Black Elk, recounted his great vision of receiving "powers of the World" during a Sun Dance, a moment in which his grandfathers gave him "a flowering stick...that was alive...and sprouted from the top and sent forth branches, and in the branches many leaves came out and murmured and in the leaves the birds began to sing. 'It shall stand in the centre of a nation's circle,' said the Grandfather, 'a cane to walk with and a people's heart; and by your powers you shall make it blossom.' "[31] In Poitras' work about the Sun Dance, *Rock Hearts* (1988), the single tree is potently absent.

Poitras' *Rock Hearts* underlines the empowerment of a native voice. On one level it refers to emancipation through the continuing ceremony of the Sun Dance. Its imaging of meditative life-sized sun dancers suggests an altered state of consciousness induced by the ritual piercing of the chest; it evokes eventual escape from earthly bonds. On a second level, *Rock Hearts* lays claim to a self-defined narrative continuity of history and identity evoked through the materially absent flowering stick, the single tree. *Rock Hearts*, to invoke Clifford's phrase, is about textualization, "a process through which unwritten behaviour, speech, beliefs, oral tradition, and ritual come to be marked as a corpus, a potentially meaningful ensemble separated out from an immediate discursive or performative situation."[32] Textualization is a tie to history, and the basis through which land claims might be made. Poitras' exploration of new texts for the exhibition would, in a radically activist sense, "put other cultural realities in jeopardy"; in a textual sense, a sense more remote yet no less profound, he creates himself as a new subject. As he discovers his place within a tradition and the experience of a people, Poitras both places himself within a historical narrative, and places Europeans within its construct too. He assumes the stance of the postcolonial, the stance of one who uses a history of colonization to return the gaze on those who would name him the other. Rather than assimilation, he asserts hybridization, a form of cultural synthesis in which, he notes, "we have all drawn lines of defense for the recognition and acceptance of our difference."[33] Poitras characterizes European settlers not so much in the terms of a cultural relativism — that is, an identity constructed in relation to his own — but rather in a narrative that begins with an assertion of Indian history. "My interior is Indian Territory," Poitras writes, "and my Manifest Destiny is the recovery of history for your assimilation."[34]

Poitras deconstructs the essentialist position: they are not us, we are not the other. His continuing references to an Indian history answer the constructed and constituted European history of settlement in the "New World." By placing himself in the midst of *Rock Hearts*, for example, Poitras accepts Indian history as his own. And yet, one of the four figures images a white man invited into the Indian ritual. It is a new meeting ground, within Indian history and upon a middle ground

32. Clifford, 37.

33. Edward Poitras and Matthew Teitelbaum, *Indian Territory* (Saskatoon: Mendel Art Gallery, 1988), 24.

34. Ibid., 25.

which now shifts for Europeans, too. "What is seen by the mainstream is only the tip of the cultural iceberg," Poitras declares, "its totality submerged in a cloak of silence. The surface is your deception, and it is we who are watching you."[35]

III

Two worlds: In one, Black Elk's requiem of 1931: "There is no centre any longer, and the sacred tree is dead." In the other, just three years later, Arthur Lismer's invocation of the lone pine tree in Tom Thomson's *The West Wind* as the "spirit of Canada made manifest in a picture." One, a call to revive native tradition and reverse the ravages of history; the other a statement of belief in nationhood, universalism, and the potency of shared values. For the Group of Seven, if not for Black Elk, connectedness to the land was actualized in the act of painting, an expressionist and emotive projection backed up by the assurance of securely established cultural values. Implicit in a link between nationhood and the representation of place is a belief in the symbolic power of images to stand for a shared actual experience. The symbolic function of an image is encapsulated in an ornamental function which memorializes that experience.

Now, the possibility of a new world: Poitras' world, or a world in which the privileges of a colonial order are crumbling. It is a world in which the values of the established populations, and the symbols which image their claims to authority, cannot hold. It is the new world of the changing metropolis and the changing hinterland, of the postcolonial, of the migrant, of the seemingly never-ending movement of peoples, in Salman Rushdie's phrase, a world of "black, brown and white leaking into one another." Literary theorist Homi Bhabha has written of this emerging moment. "The postcolonial perspective," Bhabha writes, "forces us to rethink the profound limitations of a consensual and collusive 'liberal' sense of community. It insists — through the migrant metaphor — that cultural and political identity is constructed through a process of otherness."[36] Community in the postcolonial construct is not geographically centred, nor defined by nation-states. Indeed, in its relation to the colonial moment, postcolonialism asks retrospectively of the colony and empire relation, in what sense

35. Ibid., 24.

36. Homi Bhabha, "Novel Metropolis," *The New Statesman*, 16 February 1990, 16.

does community exist when it is defined by subjugation? In the postcolonial moment, the question is asked: "How are the forms and effects of an older colonial consciousness [re-written and re-interpreted] from the later experience of migration, diaspora and cultural displacement that marks the recent, post-war histories of the Western metropolis?"[37] In the Canadian context, the composite other realizes itself in both a new world of immigrants and shifting populations — more than 185,000 immigrants entering Canada in 1989, more than 13,500 claiming refugee status under new Canadian immigration laws — and a reawakened sense of the inherent rights of native peoples concerning land claims, ethical rights, historical knowledge.

It is clear that in an age of settlement and resettlement, of fluidity of populations and contrast in the symbols which partially materialize them, traditional coding practices may be increasingly questioned. Nature-based images need not simply be "out there," existing as idealized projections about rural life and space. Histories of colonial empires have radically altered our sense of landscape as neutral territory. Raymond Williams, for example, has shown that we cannot name the countryside as an idealized site of settlement, of community instilled cooperation, and community encouraged productivity.[38]

Even though much of his own experience of *country* marked his thought, Williams argued against any heroizing of the rural experience; for him, it was tied to the heaves and sputters of the capitalist system, the history of the metropolis and its extended divisions of land. "Indeed," Williams wrote,

> as the persistent concentration of ownership, first of the land, then of
> all the major means of production, was built into a system and a state,
> with may kinds of cultural and political mediation, it was easy for the
> perception to diminish though the fact was increasing. Many modern
> ruralists, many urban conservationists, see "the state" or "the plan-
> ners" as their essential enemy, when it is quite evident that what the
> state is administering and the planners serving is an economic system
> which is capitalist in all its main interiors, procedures and criteria.[39]

Williams' argument against the capitalist system, and the dichotomy between country and city which it provokes, is extended in his consideration of the strategies of

37. C.L.R. James, paraphrased in Bhabha, 16.

38. Raymond Williams, *The Country and the City* (New York: Oxford University Press, 1973), 279–306.

39. Ibid., 294.

Rodney Graham
Millenial Project for an Urban Plaza 1986
architectural model
Collection: Vancouver Art Gallery
Photo: Jim Jardine

colonialism. For Williams, the colonial empire extends the capitalist system; it allows Britain, for example, to become a predominantly industrial and urban society. New industrial production became a massive export, and the colonies became a supplier of raw material — they were invented as the "new" countryside. Further, emigration to the colonies served as a solution to the poverty and overcrowding of the cities, providing an escape valve to keep the cities sane. It was the route, after all, of thousands of rural workers already displaced by the reordered economy of postindustrialized Britain. In her nineteenth-century novel, *Mary Barton,* Elisabeth Gaskell concludes by bringing her heroine to Canada, in Williams' phrase, "in a mood of rural idyll and escape as powerful as any of the earlier English images."[40]

In his 1988 text on the work of fellow Vancouver artist Rodney Graham, Jeff Wall wrote of the particular place the single tree might hold in the iconography of the city:

> Rarely do we see an isolated tree in the city. The reason for this is profoundly ideological. The lone tree is the great ancient symbol of the mortal individual, rooted in the totality of nature yet suffering its solitary destiny. In an epoch when the totality of nature begins to suffer mortally, we begin to see it as an individual. In this the totemic and wholistic vision of tribal, aboriginal cultures is re-recognized by non-Natives as scientific truth.... In this epoch, a tree standing self-consciously alone in the city would, better than any other monument or form of propaganda, evoke the environmental tragedy which indicts our economy, our culture of cities, our social order.[41]

And so, renewed lament for the destruction of a past is re-formed as a critique of the ravages of capital excess. Graham's single tree, whether the subject of *Millenial Project for an Urban Plaza* (1986), or of the serial work *Flanders Trees* (1989), extends Williams' argument, for these single trees are neither country nor city trees, they are realized in a traverse in between. The tree is the subject of exchange, the implicated subject in a causal relation. The solitary tree in *Millenial Project* assumes its role as a cautionary tale in its relation to the specific environmental devastations logging has wreaked upon the British Columbia landscape. It is set within an inner city urban plaza as a site of pronouncement and accusation, in purposeful proximity to any one of the all-knowing, wood-panelled head offices

40. Ibid., 281.

41. Jeff Wall, "Into the Forest," *Rodney Graham* (Vancouver: Vancouver Art Gallery, 1988), 16.

of multinational logging conglomerates. The tree is projected into an imagined future in *Millenial Project* not to negate its function as a natural resource but to herald its sensitive role in the ecosystem of a place. The country as site is implicated explicitly in the economic structures determined at the centre.

Rather than marker of site, the tree is a marker of resonance between sites. The trees in *Flanders Trees* (1989) are inverted, marking an end to neutral transactions with an idealized nature. The trees are neither specific in their geographic reference (they are actually Belgian trees) nor rooted to place. It denies, therefore, its historically-grounded reading, that is, as a tree of the country, of the wilderness, of homogeneous community. Graham's tree is a complex sign, at once an interrogation of a landscape encapsulated by the codified geometries of territorialization *and* an acknowledgement of such control. In his bookwork, *The System of Landor's Cottage* (1987), Graham described a landscape enclosed within a labyrinthian architecture. Man-made artifice was a measure of control. In its form of presentation, *Flanders Trees* (1989) suggests artifice as indictment. The series of five prints, and white gloves for their handling, are enclosed in a wooden presentation case. The case is made of cedar. In time, the acid it releases will corrode the photographic prints and obliterate their image.

In the colonial construct, the isolated tree marked the boundary between place of being and place of desire. The tree at the horizon marked only a midpoint in a presumed discovery and naming of a potential paradise. In the postcolonial construct, the solitary tree assumes various, though related masks. It is transformed in Bill Reid's Skidegate totem poles; it is absent in Edward Poitras' Sun Dance flowering stick; it is inverted in Rodney Graham's oaks and elms. In all instances, it is detached and rootless. It neither marks a specific claim to territory nor a site of individual possession, yet it insistently inscribes experience and affirms presence. The single tree, in its postcolonial construction, reclaims history in this moment, reclaims the landscape as its stage.

ROBERT FONES
Erratics Train

Erratics

Train

Erratics Train

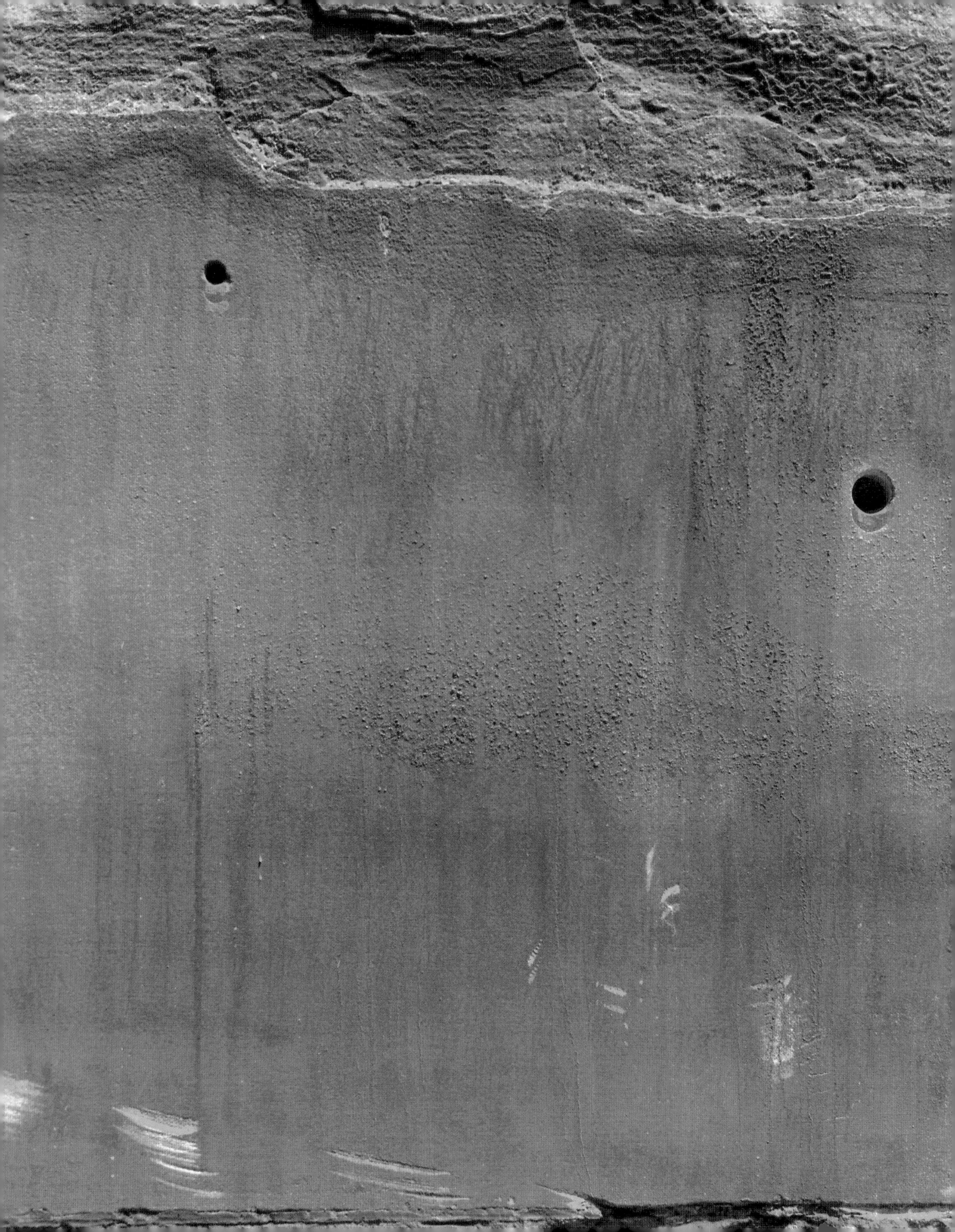

DISFIGURED NATURE:
THE ORIGINS OF THE
MODERN CANADIAN LANDSCAPE

Scott Watson

The metaphor between land and body (usually female) is as old as literature. In the mythos of Western societies, nature is clearly female and the exploration of her is accordingly patriarchal. One might expect to find evidence of the patriarchal narrative in landscape painting, where the subject is often nature. Paintings of unpeopled mountains, fields, streams and forests do show, however, traces of social human bodies — bodies that are highly contested sites, circumscribed by regulation and legislation. Land or territory, which is also the subject of landscape painting, is more obviously the site of regulation and legislation about use and ownership. Yet, these two topics on which any landscape painting might be expected to speak, the social body and the physical land, are not always distinguishable. The seemingly innocent terms of a metaphorical and poetic discourse often burst with great violence into social reality.

The landscape, as a particularly European form of representation and genre painting, is tied to the rise of mercantile capitalism. While a tradition of art historical and critical writing imagines landscape painting as an enactment of a philosophical discourse about nature and culture, the genre may also be seen to document the administration and ownership of land. In modern times, especially in Canada, national and racial values are embedded deeply in the imagination of land or territory as it is represented in landscape painting. In these terms, nature as the subject of a picture has many subtexts besides the romantic one usually foregrounded. The landscape tradition in Canada depends on a multitude of descriptions which have vied for authenticity and truth. Key among these is the term *wilderness*. In his recent controversial judgement on the Gitskan and Wet'suwet'an land claims in British Columbia, which denied the legitimacy of those claims, Judge Alan McEachern described the territory in question as "a vast emptiness." That this "emptiness" is otherwise described as a plenitude of natural resources by the same powers that legitimize the court was an irony that escaped the judge. *Nature, natural, wilderness,* and *emptiness* are all familiar terms in Canada's cultural production where they are usually deployed to describe something essential about the country and the psyche of its citizens. These terms, in

Group of Seven image in circulation:
Tom Thomson
The Drive 1916–17
Collection: University of Guelph/Macdonald
Stewart Art Centre
Photo: Cheryl Bellows

1. Fred Housser, *A Canadian Art Movement: The
Story of the Group of Seven* (Toronto: Macmillan,
1926), 125.

view of the historical struggle over ownership, administration and self-determination of the First Nations people, are terms that distribute power by imaging a pre-economic, unnamed, unmapped and largely uninhabited world.

The Group of Seven painters represent a case in point. Their wild nature is suspect, always one step ahead of the timber licence: they portrayed a nature they knew was disappearing. Indeed, rather than resist the onslaught of resource exploitation, they hoped that posterity would reward them for leaving a record of a disappearing wilderness. In an odd way, they almost seemed to reckon that the moment the evidence (that is, their inspirational motif) was gone, the paintings would come into their own. They deliberately set out to paint the past for the future. They imagined the wild as unpeopled, unexplored and untravelled except by that remote other, the native Indian. It seems all the more pertinent now, in light of renewed crises over native land claims to recognize that the Group's wilderness is politicized, disputed territory and that a prior cultural claim to their landscape is utterly suppressed and hidden in their painting.

I. The War Dead: The Male Landscape of the Group of Seven

Guided by the American poet, Walt Whitman, the Group also drew on the energies of the war with its repressive enforcement of strictly heterosexual male bonding. The painting that resulted expressed a mythical nature — patriarchal, romantic, sexual — through which the importance of the body as a subtext in the formation of modern Canadian landscape painting is revealed.

Walt Whitman, ecstatic nature nationalist, was Merlin to the Group's band of sacred knights. Whitman's hypnotic, exclamatory poetry revolves around the same axes as the vision of the Group: nature, the war dead and the creation of a heroic race consciousness. The movement's originative hero, Tom Thomson, had been "taken" by nature in 1917.[1] The death of Thomson was tinged with Wagnerism; it consummated his affair with the wild and the untamed. The search for nature by the Group after Thomson's death became a search for his spirit as well, for he had become part of "her." Thomson's death in the wild could be contrasted with the carnage of the First World War. In a way, this solitary death in the wild was on the same continuum as the deaths in the trenches of Europe; it was an intoxicant for the living, and a kind of necessary sacrifice. "The long lists of casualties published in the daily newspapers added fuel to the national spirit," wrote Fred Housser who saw the potential of transferring the "swell of national feeling" awakened by war to the creation of race consciousness through the imagination of the North as mediated by the Group. As Housser, author of *A Canadian Art Movement* claimed, when "the stimulus of struggle had been withdrawn," the "creative and magnificent communion" with nature could continue to "stir the national pulse" at wartime pitch through painting.[2] In this context, the subject of the Group, especially Algonquin Park where Thomson died, is not nature at all, but the spirit world of the dead heroes, Valhalla.

Painting the war prepared the Group for painting Canada's landscape, just as the blood sacrifice of war prepared the scene for the birth of the Canadian race. Usually thought of as unpeopled, the classic visionary paintings of the North in fact, are haunted with spirits. The legions of war dead, the martyred petulant boy painter and nature mystic, Tom Thomson and the somnolent body of the male collective are all to be found in the northern woods and lakes. A consummation with nature also represents a mystical male bonding with these dead Aryan brethren. The autumn flames of Algonquin's woods are the funeral pyres of heroes, the red maple leaf an emblem of a slain soldier's brave heart. It was the secret and sacred heart of the forest and the object of the annual autumn quest: "Every day advanced the passing of the leaf and soon our painters had to go in quest of the desirable spot of red."[3]

II. Fondling in the Wild

The difference between the eroticism of Whitman and that of the Group, vastly contrasting in their heat of expression, is one of degrees of sublimation. Whitman loves the young soldier ("O strong dead-march you please me!") openly, passionately, scandalously. The romantic yearning in Housser's book is for a boy scout

Group of Seven images in circulation:
Arthur Lismer
A September Gale 1921
Collection: The National Gallery of Canada, Ottawa
Photo: Cheryl Bellows

4. Ibid., 51.

5. O.J. Firestone, *The Other A.Y. Jackson: A Memoir* (Toronto: McClelland and Stewart, 1979), 185.

sort of male bonding that has been given the additional colouration of the Gothic homoeroticism of the official and popular celebrations of the war dead. Certainly no member of the Group had the capacity for feeling or the imagination to understand the erotic currents of the war culture in which they began to construct their northern Valhalla. Aspects of *A Canadian Art Movement* are suggestive of an erotic dynamic in a dreamy, anaemic sort of way, such as this passage on nibbling and tickling: "Beauty lives lonely like a sleeping angel in the lap of the soul. At first only suspected or felt in little breath-blown stirrings, like long spears of grass in ever-so-little nibbles of a breeze. Yet that which is so gentle has power to drive a man through all but overpowering circumstances to an end which in the beginning, is only vagueness, but clarifies like dawn."[4]

Sexual identity and libidinal economy concerned the Group and they wove these concerns into their work and the construction of themselves as legendary painters. O.J. Firestone, a biographer of A.Y. Jackson described, somewhat painfully, Jackson's assessment of Thoreau MacDonald in these words: "Even though he was a bachelor, Alex used to feel sorry for men who missed all female company. One of the occupants of the Studio Building was Thoreau MacDonald, the son of J.E.H. MacDonald, a good friend and fellow member of the Group of Seven. Thoreau was a shy person who led a lonely life. On one occasion when he seemed quite grouchy, Alex remarked to Harris in fun that Thoreau would be a happier person if he had a woman's company. 'All he needed,' Alex said, 'was a good fuck.'"[5] In his search for Jackson's sexual life, Firestone operates within the dominant grid. He gathers the gossip to construct another Jackson and effectively dispels any suspicion of homosexuality that usually hangs over bachelors by pointed but sad portrayals of the old artist's heterosexual liaison. Firestone presumes that "a woman's company" and "good fuck" are synonymous, interchangeable terms in a syntax everyone understands. This is the given view of a heterosexual man and an abiding law of the patriarchy.

A good deal of the myths generated by the Group of Seven involved a discourse about gender and sexual orientation. Housser's fundamental text is shot through

Title page ornament from *A Canadian Art Movement* by Fred Housser ©1926, published by Macmillan of Canada, a Division of Canada Publishing Corporation. Artist: Thoreau MacDonald

6. Housser, 15.

7. Ibid., 16.

8. Ibid., 24.

9. Ibid., 117.

with notions of virility and masculinity which in turn become the key components in the construction of the authentically Canadian artist. The European model of the decadent polysexual dandy is renounced. The painter of the Canadian landscape "divests himself of the velvet coat and flowing tie of his caste, puts on the outfit of the bushwhacker and prospector; closes with his environment; paddles, portages and makes camp; sleeps in the out-of-doors under the stars; climbs mountains with his sketch box on his back," in order to discover that "virgin mood unchastened by contact with man."[6] The tradition of European art is demonized by Housser as "that beautifully powerful despot" who "gets into the saddle of the soul and curbs for at least a time the freest spirit."[7] In short, the Canadian artist confronts the new land face to face, while the traditions of Europe mount from behind.

Shaking off the European tradition requires a "direct contact with Nature herself."[8] While the guiding narrative of Housser's book is a spiritual quest for national values and race consciousness, his subtext is a search for virility. The idea of manliness is realized in the contact with virgin nature. But nature in this regard was a complicated construction. Nature was female, virgin and unchastened, yet there was an androgynous aspect to her. The Group of Seven painter is chaste in the wild. He takes no female companion there and finds no native princess or prince in the woods, only "that sweet loneliness which is exaltation."[9] Jackson's bachelorhood, as Firestone unwittingly points out, was necessarily a part of the legend. He was spoken for, married to his motif, just as the tortured nature worshipper Tom Thomson had been. The Group's Valhalla was a male domain. Knights errant in the woods, but decked out in business suits in Toronto, the Group was enchanted with nature's curative powers, its ability to heal the wounds of war and restore manhood to the depleted nation.

Thoreau MacDonald, he-in-need-of-a-good-fuck, designed the title page ornament for *A Canadian Art Movement*. A mystic emblem combining triangle and circle, the design depicts the solitary tree rising from a wild lily blossom, a sacrificial male organ giving birth to the empowered erect tree as a symbol of male progenesis. "It is an allegorical tree," Housser wrote of Lismer's

Gale: "In it he has gathered up the epic spirit of innumerable great trees which have been wounded by storms and healed themselves again."[10]

Although mother nature is female in the poetic cosmos of the West, the Group established a view of nature that was replete with masculine attributes, as if it were the sacred refuge of manhood itself. Pulsing rhythms, cataracts and streams were signs of a virile and self-regenerating energy that more than once in Housser's text is imagined as the tap source for a protean capitalism which would be the instrument for disseminating the Group's aesthetic throughout Canadian experience. In turn, the Group's view of nature provided the appropriate perspective for further exploration and exploitation.

As the Group's landscape images spread across the country via the medium of silkscreen reproductions designed for the post office and school room, they became enmeshed in a symbolism of a different order. Reduced to icons in the flat, matte colours of silkscreen, they became signs of obedience to a bureaucracy that had appropriated the Group myth to the extent that their images stood simply for the state order.

10. Ibid., 181.

III. Watersports

However much Group of Seven images oppressed school children and government workers, the Group members acted as individual touchstones to the fount of Canadian modernism, as living contacts to the country's early unhappy marriage to the twentieth century. Futurism, cubism, constructivism and Dada flourished in Europe amidst modernity's crisis, while Canadians thought modernity was a picture of Algonquin Park. Although Group followers included prominent women painters, none could be admitted into the sacred brotherhood itself. It was the male painter who could pass on the tradition and impart its phallic mysteries. As one student (male) described Fred Varley, who took the Group's message to Vancouver in the twenties, this most satyr-like member of the Group was seen as the conduit of a natural force, almost a kind of phallus himself: "We first imagined Varley to be a self-primed fount of knowledge, but we soon discovered that he was a spout

here transposed it, silhouetting its wind-worn shape before
the infinite horizon line and the great rolling layers of
clouds. We can recognize the broad-based triangular composition, and the light breaking from the upper left corner,
both effects explored earlier in *Miners' Houses, Glace Bay.*
Linking horizontal areas of sky, clouds, lake, rock and

still progre
1917, was i
the First W
revolution,
pendent Ca
and the oth
this advance
So Jack
applying th
went, until
the Group
ducing dec
rooms. Ma
Rocky Mou
more and n
a teacher, a
edge of ou
coast lectu
of children
September
Even wl
ning in 192
ing their b
tions with
made such
Then in
force in the

Fig. 133:   Lawren Harris, *North Shore, Lake Superior,*
1926, oil, 40" x 50", National Gallery

Group of Seven image in circulation:
Lawren Harris
North Shore, Lake Superior 1926
Collection: The National Gallery of Canada, Ottawa
Photo: Cheryl Bellows

11. Fred Ames, unpublished lecture cited by J.
Russell Harper, *Painting in Canada: A History,*
Second Edition (Toronto: University of Toronto
Press, 1978), 284.

through which flowed all the excitement of the world, spiced rather than tamed by sound aesthetic training. It was a violent stream that was hosed on us, but these roots were nourished even if some washed away; and it was a directed steady stream."[11] Not many of the little treelets fertilized by the steady stream that hosed from Varley's spout outgrew their experience of his vision. The artist who gained most from the Group was not a Varley student, nor a man.

IV. Disinterrment

Emily Carr produced, late in her life, a body of work that was stimulated and encouraged by the Group, particularly by Lawren Harris. Her paintings remain among the most sexualized of any Group or Group-influenced artist. She never tired, in work after work, of paying homage to the vitalism she not only believed she perceived in nature but which she also thought was appropriate to a modern idiom. Her spiritual guide to nature was also the gay bard, Walt Whitman. In her paintings, nature is rendered symbolic: trees are giant male organs and forest byways, orifices for penetration, the sky and sea tingle with the universal vibration. Her landscapes are also haunted, not with the war dead, but with ruins of other civilizations. In her paintings, the fecundity of nature overwhelms old totem poles and renews itself amidst the slash of logged culls. One would not claim that Carr consciously sought to define the terms of this conflict in her work, nor can we count her as an environmental activist in the contemporary sense. She created an imaginary nature, thinking she was disclosing its source of truth. While she eventually abandoned the patriarchal vocabulary of the Group, her life's work involved the presentation of the ruins rather than the living fabric of First Nations people. The rapport she sought with the ruins and the allegorical narrative of "nature-conquers-all" eclipsed the possibility of any understanding of the social, political and cultural struggles that are involved in the territories she depicted. Thus while her work rebelled against the conventions of painting and in her life she rebelled against the conventions of a patriarchal society, her work insisted that nature was an expression of God. She seemed to have little knowledge of the real legislative oppressions of her First Nations friends and encouraged the view that they were part of natural, rather than human, history.

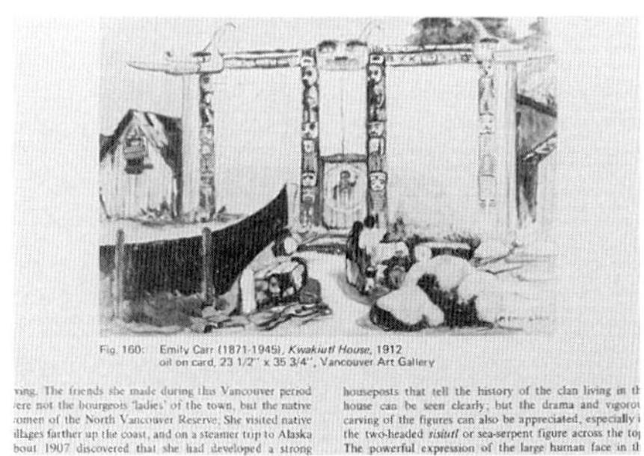

Emily Carr
Kwakiutl House 1912
Collection: Vancouver Art Gallery
Photo: Cheryl Bellows

The view of nature that emerges from the aesthetic program of the Group is a stage set for the patriarchal ghost. Carr's nature was the result of a projection of poetic vitalism on forests, skies and growing things. She liked instability, hated civilization and saw in the forces of natural regeneration a kind of utopian nihilism and the potential end of what men had made. Carr's ruins are carcass-like; there's a sense of something violated, a body disinterred, of something brought wrongly into the corrosive light and air. This morbidity in her was stimulated and fueled by the idea of cultural extinction and annihilation and she sought the evidence among old abandoned village sites and falling totems, using them as an allegory for the vanity of all male construction.

The middle-class cult of Emily Carr tends to obscure the challenging negation her paintings often imply. Her biographers, perhaps like Carr herself, have declined to deal with her sexuality. There are no records of her sexual or erotic attachments; she may have had none. The idea of sex seemed to disgust her. The view that Carr was lonely and sexually frustrated (incomplete) has been voiced by her biographers and friends. Some attribute this to an early affair gone wrong, family trauma (we'd say abuse these days), others to Carr's own sense that, as a woman, she could never marry and remain independent enough to realize her art (yet she put art on the back burner for fifteen years). Her work and her personality have been appropriated by the very normative culture she rebelled against. Speculation about her sexuality revolves around the terms of lack, repression and unfullfilment. It is always a heterosexual lack, however, that is under scrutiny. None discuss Carr's unrealized potential for lesbian relationships. Thus sexism and homophobia still circumscribe an understanding of her work, and thus an understanding of her vitalist readings of nature. For example, when she dropped the hard phallicism Lawren Harris had encouraged for her late manner of rhythmic vibrations, was she attempting to define her motif as an expression of a feminine sensibility? Her choice to abandon form and mass for a vision of continuous movement was an attempt to discover transcendent unities. Nevertheless, this decision also meant an end to her readings of nature as a phallic, heterosexual allegory of thrall and penetration in favour of a reading of unfettered movement and corresponding vibrations.

V. Dismembering the Body

One of the few painters to work through the Group aesthetic and arrive at a modern, eroticized painting based on nature is Jack Shadbolt. He knew Carr as a young man when he and so many of his contemporaries read Housser's *A Canadian Art Movement* as a call to artistic commitment. His mature work, coming from his postwar explorations of abstract expressionism, became deeply involved with nature as a metaphor for inner psychic states and sexual drives. In his work, phallic form is represented in a state of crisis. It is constantly subject to disintegration from forces within and without. And Shadbolt's work oscillates between depictions of fields of energy and dismembered form. Members of the Group touched on similar motifs — Varley constructed an allegory of sado-masochism — but as abstractions of history, Shadbolt's paintings carry on the tradition of Carr, albeit without the drive for transcendental feeling.

Shadbolt is not a landscape painter, he paints nature. Like Carr he is fascinated with decrepitude and stung with colonial and cultural anxieties which he displays in his use of the art of First Nations people. In a search for roots he concocts a compost of old masks and carvings: leavened by the rain forest, this becomes the fertile ground for the colonial/colonist to create a new indigenous modernism. As with the Group, this project is related to a response to war, except Shadbolt's war dead are the victims of the camps of the Second World War. Images of a sawed-off tree stump and a soldier's amputated limb exist on the same continuum, revealing a paradigmatic modern form. In these images, nature is a void. It is both the inner emptiness of the transplanted alienated modern and the interstellar emptiness of his cosmos; it represents the nothingness between subatomic particles and the purposelessness of modern atheistic life.

VI. Whose Body? Prescriptions for the Embodied Landscape

The trajectory that begins with Tom Thomson and finds its climax in postwar nature abstraction — of which Shadbolt is perhaps the most interesting example — involves a narrative of the body. In this history the landscape is a graveyard for

the heroes of war, but it is a graveyard that must be disturbed and violated. Those
that came before have to be disinterred before the land can be truly owned. This
ghoulish project tinges the host of other repressions, crypto-fascism and imperial-
ist dreams that define Canadian modernism with its pallor and palpable panic
when confronted with nature or sex. The primary conflict which must inform
every attempt to paint a Canadian landscape is about ownership and fundamental
claims of sovereignty. This theme is at the base of every notion of wilderness — a
notion that depends for its dynamic on the invisibility of the First Nations and a
national historical forgetting of the injustices done to them. Nature in Canadian
art, or indeed, in Canada, will always be disfigured by history, unless, perhaps one
day there is both justice and remembering.

EDWARD POITRAS

Relocating Tribes

ENGLISH

FRENCH

SPANISH

THE
ACCIDENTAL
TOURIST

Maureen P. Sherlock

The economic vanguard of late capital continues to transform all the traditional paradigms with which we have assayed our domesticated world. As the captains of Western culture have shifted their focus from the sphere of exploration and exploitation to the corporate boards of cultural production, once familiar categories of art, science and philosophy have also undergone a radical transformation. I wish to examine both the past and present prevailing character of our relationship to a landscape disguised as nature in our pursuit of authentic experience, restoration theologies and pastoral rambles. I do so to better grasp the counter-strategies deployed by contemporary artists seeking to expose the truth of nature as a pawn of history.

While some artists are content to reproduce the social relations of the present or evoke the nostalgia of lost innocence, there remain others whose work either challenges the determinism of ideology, or retrieves a silenced past as a weapon with which to address the future. Nowhere is this more clear than in contemporary art issues of borderlands, countrysides and city-sights. Interventionist strategies, like those of Dennis Adams, Jenny Holzer, Krzysztof Wodiczko, Group Material, Alfredo Jaar and Lothar Baumgarten, abound in urban way-stations to dislodge the convenient meanings of social space. Recent critical discourse has also been mesmerized by the metropolis with its spectacle of unnatural light. Our retrieve of the work of Guy Debord, Walter Benjamin and Henri Lefebvre, our fascination with mid-nineteenth-century Paris, popular entertainment and semiotics, as well as the recent work of Susan Buck-Morss, T.J. Clark and Andreas Huyssen, all mark a renewed focus on quotidian life and its loss of revolutionary potential.

Urban theory, however, is also witnessing the return of the referent to the gates of the city, the resistance of an invasive nature to the fantasia of our Disneylands. Nowhere is it described better than in Sartre's *Nausea:*

> I am afraid of cities. But you musn't leave them. If you go too far you
> come up against the vegetation belt. Vegetation has crawled for miles
> towards the cities. Once the city is dead the vegetation will cover it, will
> climb over the stones, grip them, search them, make them burst with its
> long black pincers;...You must stay in the cities as long as you are alive,
> you must never penetrate alone this great mass of hair which lies at the

gates....In the cities, if you know how to take care of yourself, and choose times when all the beasts are sleeping in their holes and digesting, behind the heaps of organic debris, you rarely come across anything more than minerals, the least frightening of all existents.[1]

Nature as death is no longer a purely cultural category in the face of AIDS, hospital waste littering oil-covered shorelines, forests destroyed by acid rains and a pattern of global warming that threatens the immutability of tropic geography. Sartre's description of Bouville is imbued with the sensibility of an over-civilized Europe. When he speaks of minerals as the least frightening of all existents, we know he has never seen a strip mine.

These eco-events mark a shift in the balance of rhetorical power between nature and culture as they collapse the categories so carefully laid by idealist philosophies of science, including structuralism and some high altitude versions of deconstruction. What Heidegger once called "the precursory resistance of Being," a density not subsumable by calculative thinking haunts the rain forests and the timberlands with a deadly silence. In the face of our exploitation of the earth, it is difficult to conceive of the landscape within the eighteenth-century European sensibilities of the beautiful, the sublime and the picturesque. I propose to examine these earlier concepts in light of their recent theoretical and historical reappraisal in the postmodern theory of tourism.

As a fundamental premise for understanding English landscape painting, Ann Bermingham proposes:

> Rustic landscape painting is ideological in that it presents an illusory account of the real landscape while alluding to the actual condition existing in it....Because an artist's connection to dominant class ideologies is never simple, art is capable of showing contradictions within the various ideological functionings of the superstructure...art sets itself in a dialogical relation to specific ideologies, it betrays its own ideological underpinnings...though it produces ideology and exists within it, it also registers the inconsistencies within ideologies and pinpoints the places where their totalizing worldview threatens to unravel....[2]

1. Jean-Paul Sartre, *Nausea*, trans. Lloyd Alexander (New York: New Directions, 1959), 208–9.

2. Ann Bermingham, *Landscape and Ideology: the English Rustic, 1740–1860* (Berkeley: University of California Press, 1989), 3–4.

While I substantively agree with her thesis, I will extend it to a wider range of contemporary art projects. Tourism and the techniques of modern reproduction have transformed the analysis of the traditional supra/infra structure in market and monopoly capital. Though there is an uneven development world wide, North America is most certainly at the third or consumer stage of capital. Leisure and culture no long represent a reflecting mirror to economic relations, they have become the major force of the production of desire and consumption.

European landscape art since the Renaissance has been marked by three often overlapping tropes: first, the rhetoric of uninhabited aesthetic *sights* which masks entrepreneurial intentions; second, elegiac *citations* of abandoned pasts or desired manifest destinies; and last, the mapping of *sites* for future exploration and economic exploitation. All three categories finally collapse exhausted into the landscape of tourism. While panoramic scenes from the jungle paintings of Heade to Watkin's photographs of Yosemite Valley are touted as aesthetically beautiful for their own sake, we often fail to examine their ideological effect of visually depopulating the territories they display. Transforming a native people's *habitat* into an empty space awaiting "liberation" by white culture, artists often prepared the way for the *real* elimination of tribal culture. Artists, after all, generally accompanied commercial or military expeditions, and were instrumental in estab-lishing colonialist imperatives and exoticized foreign landscapes. Here beauty is not so much in the eyes of the beholder as it is in the domineering projects of a blind colonialist ambition. Beauty here cloaks the political and economic objec-tives of a certain class, race and gender to the detriment or exclusion of others.

It is this same Kantian concept of the beautiful that dominates both the formalist aesthetics of Clement Greenberg and Jurgen Habermas' communicative totality. It is the aesthetic of high modernism, *par excellence,* but not that of Dada and surre-alism with their disruptive tactics. It claims, rather, a critical universality of taste that creates a bridge over very troubled waters. In earlier critiques Kant had se-vered a totalizing scientific knowledge from any connection to the absolute moral precept which alone could transcend custom and attain a ground for international law. This shattered the community of truth and justice into the separated spheres of scientific knowledge and moral or political life, each with their own rules and scenarios.

Kant offered us an aesthetic of the beautiful that would create on the level of feeling what was impossible in the orders of knowledge and desire, science and civil life. Beauty offered the middle class an imaginary reconciliation to a progressively more alienated life under capital. What was lost in the totalizing faith of the Middle Ages was recuperated in the stability of Hilton Kramer's religion of art, a new criterion of universal Western humanist values. The aesthetic anaesthetized the bourgeoisie, allowing for that harmony with the world and others rendered utopian by the Industrial Revolution. Distanced and detached, a subjective universality offers pleasure and satisfaction to the common sense "all men share," or would share once they accept the manifest destiny of Western culture. The beautiful only reproduces a confirmation of an aesthetic judgement already made, a consensus fossilized, a mirror image of a society's prevailing values. It delivers, for example, our delectation in an endless repetition of a Luminist landscape of a sea scaled to a white male body, while the ships of commerce carry the economy of art.

Artist Lothar Baumgarten attempts to reverse this hegemony by rendering visible the geographic site names given by the original inhabitants to their own landscapes, but later repressed by white colonialists. Reversing the European naming of Venezuela (little Venice), he inlaid the German pavilion at the 1984 Venice Biennale with the native names of the rivers of the Amazon Basin — Amazonas, Tapjos, Vaupes, Orinoco, Xingo, Purus and Tocantins. In doing so he wished to acknowledge the indigenous populations as still-active sign producers and not the mute other of colonialist fantasy. The right to map and to name has been tied to a history of power since Genesis. In the mid-eighties, the artist also renamed the Paris Metro stations with the history of French colonialism, rupturing the seamless flow of the city's ideology. Haussmann's beautification program for nineteenth-century Paris was accomplished with the largess of Napoleonic expansionism and the displacement of the "tasteless" working class to the suburbs.

Thomas Struth
Corso Vittorio Emanuele, Naples 1989
black and white photograph
Courtesy: Renaissance Society at the University of
Chicago

3. Dean MacCannell, *The Tourist: A New Theory of
the Leisure Class* (New York: Schocken Press,
1989).

Beauty, for Kant, is primarily a cosmopolitan taste that values an organic coherence and autonomy in the international work of art which is fundamentally graspable to the educated Western mind. Though our pleasure here does not depend on beauty's possession, its comprehension depends on membership in the class it addresses. In its quiet contemplation, we nostalgically restore a fictional sense of wholeness and social reality missing from our actual landscapes of billboards, antennae, tenements and working-class housing, as suggested in the postmodern allegories of artist Thomas Struth. Here the stillness of Luminism is transformed into an architecture of death that implodes on the viewer allowing no escape: Tokyo, Dusseldorf, Naples, New York, all interchangeable even down to the new ship of status, a Mercedes on every street corner. Struth's mock objectivity reveals the city of late capital, a nightmare photomontage beyond even Heartfield's wildest dreams. Gothic churches, renaissance halls, neoclassical court houses, international-style tenements, all butt up against one another in a chorus line production of "As Time Goes By." We assimilate these conditions within and between as natural to urban life, rather than productions of accumulation. In a global economy, all difference is levelled by the commodity form, everything is of equal gravity in the flow of the green river: owls, sequoias, real estate developers and the lumber lobby. Struth's postmodernism denies the efficacy of the mimetic and the symbolic in favour of the twice-told tale of metropolitan allegory disguised as a documentary of discontinuity. Just as an earlier picturesque painting mediated the contradiction between a collapsing rural horizon and an emerging industrial skyline, Struth's images delineate a shrinking nationalist city from the mobility of a global economic site.

Tourism has added to the parameters of our aesthetic apprehension of both nature and the world. Our perceptions have been shaped by infinite reproductions of Ansel Adams photographs, the familiar exoticism of the beautiful Taj Mahal, as well as those wonders available from Keystone View Company, VIEW-MASTER or Kodachrome. Dean MacCannell's seminal work, *The Tourist*,[3] analyzes the role these *markers* play in the constitution of a tourist sight. Guidebooks, postcards, slide shows, knick-knacks, commemorative plates, billboards, and so on all operate in a process of "site sacralization" in the new religion of tourism. First, he claims, there is the naming stage which separates this sight from similar ones; second, are the framing stages which carefully set the borders of the sight to "protect" it; third, the frame itself becomes an attraction; fourth, mechanical reproductions of the sight, like photography, themselves become valued and displayed; and finally, there is a social reproduction where the whole apparatus becomes a source of regional pride and identity. Through this process some sites become quasi-religious in character, one's visit is as necessary as bathing in the Ganges. The art world's knowledge of Walter de Maria's *Lightning Field* comes to us through dramatic photographs of the site on a summer night filled with electricity. Art penitents confer special orders upon themselves after their pilgrimage to a New Mexican field which must only disappoint in face of its romantic markers.

The Kantian concept of the sublime dominates postmodern discourse; it is the fractured, multiple moment of the historical avantgarde and postmodernism. Where beauty leads to the confirmation of a community, the sublime names the transcendence of human freedom which presents itself in those solitary experiences of the limitless. Beauty peacefully rests with form, order and law, while the sublime isolates us in a confrontation with what cannot yet be represented on the edge of the abyss, beyond the law. I am confronted with what Sartre once called "terrible freedom": it is I and not nature which sustains naturalism. The very amorphousness of the sublime promotes its fracture into an endless series of theoretical equivocations: the mathematical, the dynamic, the counter, the comic, the gothic, the uncanny, the egotistical, the historical, the romantic, to name just a few. Like Derrida's *differance*, it escapes the boundaries of each of its own definitions in a constant deferral of meaning. It exceeds our grasp at the edge of representation in a silence and a scream, an otherness which threatens our house of cards and its familiar rules of protocol.

If beauty is a formal repetition and recognition of the axioms of the cave, then the sublime is the possibility of a different future through a caricature of the present. It

Roger Minick
*Woman at Inspiration Point,
(Yosemite)* from *Sightseer Series*, 1980
colour photograph
Courtesy: the artist

4. Yves Alain-Bois, "The Sculptural Opaque,"
Substance 31, 42.

5. For an interesting discussion of this see Gary
Shapiro's "From the Sublime to the Political," *New
Literary History* 16, 213–36. Marx himself discusses this comic sublime in the absurd reality of
Louis Napoleon in the *Eighteenth Brumaire* and its
sequel, *Herr Vogt*. Marx had planned to call it *Da-
Da Vogt*, after the Algerian translator of the emper-
or and told Engels "the fact the Da-Da will puzzle
the philistines pleases me and fits well into my
system of mockery and contempt." Cited in
Shapiro, 228.

is found, for instance, in the verbal and visual punning of both the surrealists and Dadaists who undermine the stability of meaning and therefore are rejected by both the leftist Habermas and the conservative theorist Daniel Bell. Their visions of a moralizing art are tied to the Enlightenment's dream of a perfected sphere of value through reason. Inversions and puns, on the other hand, challenge the referentiality of language, and point instead to the arbitrariness and unsteadiness of naturalism. This is seen as a threat only to those who hold or wish to reclaim the political authority of a determinate system. Yves Alain-Bois has called these destabilizing strategies an aesthetic of distraction "which no longer tries to reassure the subject with an illusion of mastery, but on the contrary plays with the loss of mastery in order to force the subject to explore...a certain opacity to things."[4] Note that he stresses this moment as play. The sublime is not so much tied to some quasi-religious terror, but to the awe-filled as awfully funny, even comic.[5]

The *double entendre*, for instance, is generally considered one of the unrespectable forms of wit; it transposes meaning on the basis of slips of the tongue that undermine the clarity of language and its ability to secure reality. Roger Minick's 1980 *Sightseer Series, Yosemite National Park* plays on a number of tropes and visual puns on the sublime. This aesthetic has been the favourite category for grasping those romantic landscapes of the self or the triumph of national destiny in our imaginary mastery of the North American continent. Minick photographs key scenic points that are framed, designated and controlled by the U.S. government park service with a sly irony revealing a once monumental nature reduced to aesthetic tropes. He reveals the earlier photographs of Watkins as the tourist items they really are by doubling the image of Yosemite Falls. The background towering valley, coded sublime by the history of photography, is dwarfed by the foreground figure of a heavy-set woman in a winter coat overlooking the site. The kerchief on her head pictures the very view she is viewing, and nature becomes another item on the tour: But if it's Tuesday, it's got to be the Grand Canyon! This sign dominates the field, the referent of nature slips back into the oblivion from which it sprang as a *memento mori* of lost horizons. A 1935 United States Park Service report reads:

Lamentable is the fact that during the six days given over to Creation,
picnic tables and fireplaces, foot bridges, toilet facilities, and many
other of man's requirements even in natural surroundings, were neg-
ligently and entirely overlooked.[6]

There is in the experience of the sublime a gap between the signified and the signifier which seems unbridgeable. As Thomas Weiskel puts it, "...the sublime began
where the conventional systems, readings of landscape or text, broke down and
found in that very collapse the foundation of another order of meaning."[7] The new
order of meaning is not founded on some aesthetic form of mysticism, but by real
material changes in our relation to nature. What is unrepresentable is tied to the
world as not-yet-spoken in the present, or barely imagined and longed for in the
future. The slippage in our reading of the landscape indicates a shift in the ideology and economics which establishes the rhetoric of its vocabulary in postmodernism. Its negative moment is to be found in the spate of apocalyptic postmodern
landscapes from Robert Morris to Anselm Kiefer, which collapse into Baudrillard's
nightmare of sublime despair. Its positive moment was the utopian aspirations of
the European avantgarde and the earth art and happenings of the 1960s.

The beginning of tourism in the British Isles coincides with the development of the
category of picturesque landscapes. It emerges toward the end of the eighteenth
century with the enclosure of the free and open pasture lands of the English countryside called commons. Estates no longer signified only peerage, but increasing
wealth and a leisured class of gentry. As new agricultural techniques produced
greater yields, the divisioned *land* signified economic value while fashionable
nature was re-invented through *landscape* gardening. Bourgeois ideology traditionally has naturalized its own supporting cultural codes to guarantee its legitimacy and necessity; gardens and landscape art are no exception to the rule.

At just those times in our history when we witness a radical change in our social
reality, we recuperate the old world through its transformation into a nostalgic,
aesthetic ideal.[8] The evocation of the countryside in the work of Gainsborough
and Constable occurs just as it is being lost to the topological parcelling of what

6. United States Park Service Report, 1935, cited
in John A. Jackle, *The Tourist: Travel in Twentieth
Century North America* (Lincoln: University of
Nebraska Press, 1985), 71.

7. Thomas Weiskel, *The Romantic Sublime* (Baltimore:
Johns Hopkins University Press, 1986), 22.

8. As professional baseball, for instance, is transformed into a scenario of postmodern profit with
contracts and franchising bids, we have been
treated to a spate of nostalgic baseball movies
glorifying an older stage of production when capital
was not as interested in sports.

was once open grazing land. As if to compensate themselves for the loss, land-
owners constructed immense gardens to restore a natural scenic view. Unlike the
formal gardens of France that are designed for a single viewing point, the rolling
views were to be seen by walking through them, thus the name *ramble*. These first
"earthworks," effected the affectation of an irregular and casual nature. It is Ann
Bermingham's thesis that this inversion allowed a reversibility between signifier
and signified, thus rendering the landscape ambiguous:

> Whereas the formal garden had stood between art and nature, the
> landscape garden tended to collapse the distinction altogether. In
> this sense, it became a *trompe l'oeil.* By conflating nature with the
> fashionable taste of the new social order, it redefined the natural in
> terms of this order and vice versa.[9]

This was a society, after all, that determined manners and etiquette as "good
breeding," so this art which disguises its artfulness should be no surprise.

9. Bermingham, 14.

Arcadian farmers in quaint pre-industrial cottages appear in painting just at the
point when agriculture in England was changing from the rural economy of the
commons and the paternalism of the feudal estate. Gardens were designed to indi-
cate our technological progress in the rational perfection of nature, while presenting ruins as signs of a lost golden age and our pastoral melancholia. Neoclassicism
is the prop of an authoritarian bourgeois politics in search of legitimacy. It is precisely this regressive politics that reappears in Ian Hamilton Finlay's Stonypath
garden in Lanarkshire, Scotland. His is a culture of pastoral moralizing to promote
the restoration of instrumental reason and the authority of enlightened empire.
One fully expects Margaret Thatcher, out for her daily constitutional amongst his
bon mots, to nod in assent to Finlay's critique of present society: "Tradition is not
dead, it has never been heard of," or "Modern sculpture is *willfully* ignorant."
Finlay offers a visual equivalent to the reactionary return-to-basics ideology of the
new conservative ideologues like Bloom and Hirsch. For those who were without
power in that tradition, such a move can only be regressive. Threatened by the
advancing forces of those the bourgeoisie never meant their revolution to fran-

chise, reactionaries everywhere look for a leader whose sense of the new order is closer to the Eighteenth Brumaire than to Nelson Mandela. Finlay's is a selective history that claims the universality of the absolute over the specificity of difference, but finally reproduces only the folly of reason. Republican virtue, like all events of great import according to Hegel, occurs twice; but as Marx claimed, "He forgot to add: the first time as tragedy, the second as farce."[10]

Michael Heizer's *Effigy Tumuli* at Buffalo Rock State Park in Ottawa, Illinois, offers an entirely different restoration than Finlay's idealism. The 200-acre site was strip mined for coal in the 1930s before the state passed laws requiring land restoration of mining sites by the responsible companies. The soil's high acidity prevented any vegetation from growing, which would have slowed the erosion of silica that leached into the Illinois River and a nearby lake. Scheduled for reclamation by state funds, the land's owners, Ottawa Silica Company, suggested and raised the money to commission Heizer for the project. The artist has always pursued a critique of European art models in his work, by appropriating both a scale and a reference commensurate with the continent's vastness and original peoples. After carefully studying the terrain, he directed the construction of earth mounds in the forms of a water strider, a frog, a catfish, a turtle and a snake. The snake, which rises from a delta in the river up a rock cliff to the plateau, is 2,070 feet long. The legs of the water strider spread over 685 feet from its gently sloped 14-foot high body.

The mounds retrieve the history of memorials to the dead built by tribal peoples in the eastern and midwestern sections of the United States which date from 100 to 500 A.D. Though frequently romanticized by colonialists and naturalists alike, the site is often read as a proof of a life integrated immediately with nature. Heizer, however, has a far more accurate and complex reading of these mounds as social testaments against an overpowering nature. The Serpent Mound of the Adena in Ohio was not covered originally with grass, but with brilliant pigments to mark their history as a people. *Effigy Tumuli* too marks a layered history of our constructions over a nature that now only exists as a form of resistance to our wills to power. The sculptures and reclamation raised more acid silica to the surface mak-

10. Karl Marx, *The Eighteenth Brumaire of Louis Bonaparte* (New York: International Publishers, 1987), 15.

Michael Heizer
Effigy Tumuli 1983–88
dirt sculpture
   foreground, Water Strider
   middleground, Frog
   background, Catfish
Photo: the artist

ing the plant growth of even acid-tolerant grasses more complex. As one walks one still sees rivulets of erosion and wonders what it means for something to be in a Rousseauian natural state. *Tumuli* offers a history to the solitary walker, but a history of overlays of which I am a part. I recall past ambulators of native Americans, coal miners, construction crews, park workers and other art tourists like myself, wondering if my footsteps are adding to the damage. My walking implicates me in an act of sustaining a certain narrative of socialized nature.

This site also points to a number of contradictions in recent developments in North American landscape art. It shares with Heizer's other work, as well as the earthworks of artists such as James Turrell, Robert Smithson, Walter de Maria and Robert Morris, a remoteness of geography and a monumentality of scale. It parallels both North America's natural wonders and such man-made phenomenon as Mount Rushmore, where man and nature are writ large. Part of the original political impetus for these works was their inability to be owned and transferred in the art economic system. As Heizer himself put it: "The position of art as malleable barter-exchange items falters as the cumulative economic structure gluts. The museums and collections are stuffed, the floors are sagging, but the real space exists."[11] Written in 1969, this quote reveals not so much the artist's naiveté as much as our general lack of critical apparatus with which to understand the operations of late capital at that time. As the economy intensified its marketing efforts in sports, leisure and culture, social reality in capital was determined more and more by these forms of production. The photographic reproductions of earthworks transform their site specificity into the abstract structure of tourist landmark.

Tourism has a deep impact on all future readings of art and its construction of nature. The English picturesque aesthetic was marked already by tourism in the Lake Country and the Highlands. By the late eighteenth century, Rowlandson already was caricaturing weary urbanites pursuing the poetry of Wales encumbered by easel, palette and sketch book. The most essential object for a tourist of the time was a Claude Glass which allowed the *perfect* point of view. Through it one could properly frame a vista and, with a full colour-range set, one also could see its seasonal changes within minutes, for you

11. Michael Heizer, "The Art of Michael Heizer," *Artforum* 8 (December 1969), 34.

might never pass this way again.[12] By the middle of the eighteenth century, colonial expansion was reified further in the widespread availability of stereo views which collapsed spatial distance. Viewers *magically* were transported to an endless series of exotic three-dimensional sights in the comfort of their own Victorian homes. The new world also saw a proliferation of engravings, chromoliths and giant dioramas that glorified the majesty of North America. The development of both canal and railway systems vastly expanded creature comforts for travel to remote geographies and exotic landscapes.

This facilitated arrival of a new figure who will shortly dominate world history — the tourist. On the heels of an entrepreneurial and expansionist capital, tourism becomes the heroic demeanour of the citizen of late capital.

It is at this juncture that the beautiful, the sublime and the picturesque find their common ground: each is reduced to a site of voyeurism and consumption. The two earlier economic stages belong in part to a classical analysis of the superstructure: an aesthetic/poetic justification for other means of production. Tourism, on the other hand, has become the singular means of production for whole communities since the beginning of the nineteenth century.

The Banff Hot Springs Reservation in Alberta, for example, was developed in 1885 not to serve an indigenous community or to protect the landscape. Part of a series of projects funded in part by the Canadian Pacific Railroad, the site was constructed solely to serve tourists. While other locales along the railroad tracks were mercilessly exploited by mining interests, Banff framed the sublime scenes of the Rockies for another kind of exploitation. After destroying many of the area's wildlife habitats, a zoo was constructed to display the endangered animals.[13] The landscape of Banff itself is in a kind of zoo, constructed and preserved for your viewing pleasure on holiday from the reality of work. As one guest put it:

> The only business at Banff is to enjoy one's self, to recreate, to loaf
> in the sunshine and worship nature. You sit at dinner in style, and
> eat your fried chicken à la Maryland to the march "El Capitan" or a
> "Fantasie From Der Freischutz" played by the Melrose Trio.[14]

12. For an excellent analysis of this topic see Malcolm Andrews, *The Search for the Picturesque* (Stanford: Stanford University Press, 1989).

13. Jackle, 82.

14. Ibid.

Hachivi Edgar Heap of Birds
billboard on the Walter Phillips Gallery 1988
outdoor installation
Photo: the artist

15. Cited in *Americans on the Road: From Autocamp to Motel, 1910–1945* (Cambridge, Mass.: MIT Press, 1981), 8.

16. Ibid., 12.

It offered the joys of an immediate nature bracketed from the mining and logging industries, while the baronial hotel designed by Bruce Price offered civilization in the heart of a nature preserve for the great white hunter who never wanted to stray too far from a Martini.

The nature of tourism changed radically in North America with the increased production of the automobile. Autocamping signified a freedom from the time schedules and hotels of the railroads. In the words of one advertisement of this time:

> You are your own master, the road is ahead; you eat as you please, cooking your own meal over an open fire; sleeping under the stars, waking with the dawn; swim in a mountain lake when you will, and always the road ahead. *Thoreau at 29 cents a gallon.*[15]

The human metaphors for the experience were tied both to native peoples and the fantasized freedom of those transplanted gypsy holdovers from the English picturesque:

> Gypsies and vagabonds, with their outcast, timeless, quasi-tragic, romantically international associations, appealed to urbane tourists who desired vacation models more sophisticated than the hunter or the trapper.[16]

Indians were archetypes for both the nomadic life and a Rousseauian restoration of North America as a preindustrial paradise for the natural man. A 1930 Santa Fe Railroad/Harveycar book called *Indian Detours* proclaims: "Those who are passing on into the setting sun made the Southwest safe for you and for us." Still it is able to assure us the sight of the native population: "Personal friendships based on mutual respect and understanding privilege us to introduce Harveycar guests to Pueblo Indian home life with an intimacy otherwise impossible." First we destroy whole civilizations, then we transform these discarded cultures into historic tourist sites. The third stage is an endless series of camp sites and motels which usurp not only native lands but their language as well by naming them after the very tribal societies they usually denied access.

Hachivi Edgar Heap of Birds, of the Tsistsistas-Cheyenne, has ruptured this tourist landscape with his *Insurgent Messages for America* series. Using articles from tourist T-shirts to billboards, he unites the parallel struggles of oppressed peoples and exposes the universal tactics of the colonizers. Comparing his work to the sharp rocks or arrowheads which made defense and preservation of native culture possible, Heap of Birds deploys a linguistic counter-strategy to combat non-Indian culture. He assaults the liberal ease that recognizes apartheid only in South Africa but not in Canada or the United States. His work's directness and assertiveness reclaims this territory of tourist travesties: "The life on the posts is always fascinating — the lounging bucks, the silent squaws and the wide-eyed children...."[17]

The tensions of postmodernism hinge on the return of a referent *who* challenges the world constructed by this imaginary tourist who colonizes the world by consuming it. Refusing the status of a "lounging buck," a real subject in history, Hachivi Edgar Heap of Birds, transforms the silent other in a vacation landscape into a word warrior of the Cheyenne Arapaho Nation.

As I watched the news this evening I saw several white Canadians shout that all Indians were animals. One even demanded that police blow up the bridge blockaded by native people in protest of treaty violations. The landscape rarely has been beautiful or sublime, for nature has always been mapped in blood.

17. *Indian Detours* (Chicago: Santa Fe System Lines and Harveycar Couriers, 1930), 46.

Daina Augaitis has been curating at the Walter Phillips Gallery in Banff, Alberta, since 1986. She is a former curator at the Western Front and Convertible Showroom in Vancouver, British Columbia.

Hans Dickel is a writer, critic and art professor in Berlin, Germany. His recent writings include a historical overview of Christina Kubisch's work for *Christina Kubisch, Orte der Zeit* (Places of Time), published by the Kunstraum München (Munich Art Gallery).

Robert Fones is a Toronto artist whose sculptures and photographic works have been exhibited throughout North America. A ten-year survey of his work was recently presented at The Power Plant in Toronto, Ontario.

David Garneau is a visual artist and critic who is co-editor of *Artichoke: writings about the visual arts*, a Calgary-based periodical.

Rodney Graham is a Vancouver-based artist whose conceptually-oriented photographs, audio, sculpture, film and bookworks have been exhibited widely throughout North America and Europe.

Christina Kubisch is a German sound artist who has exhibited throughout Europe and North America. Her installations have used electromagnetic audio transmissions to explore the paths of sound within an architecture of space.

Carroll Moppett is a Calgary-based artist and instructor at the Alberta College of Art whose work has been exhibited across Canada. Her recent investigations have considered the applications of power in Western society within a feminist context.

Helga Pakasaar is a curator of contemporary art who lives in Vancouver, British Columbia. She is a former associate curator at the Walter Phillips Gallery in Banff, Alberta.

Edward Poitras is a Regina-based artist whose work has often used text to address the role of traditional native culture in contemporary issues of self-determination. His work has been exhibited at the National Gallery of Canada and the Museum of Civilization in Ottawa and numerous galleries across Canada.

Maureen P. Sherlock was trained as a philosopher and is an associate professor of Critical Theory and Film at the School of the Art Institute of Chicago's film department. She is a regular contributor to *Arts Magazine* and *Art Papers,* for whom she edited an issue on interventionist art as social practice in January 1990. She has curated numerous shows at Randolph Street Gallery and has published extensively in a variety of journals.

Jeffrey Spalding is an active member of the Canadian art community as an artist, curator and art historian. He has developed a substantial permanent collection at the University of Lethbridge Art Gallery where he has been curating for ten years. His work has been exhibited extensively throughout the country.

Ritsuko Taho has been teaching and working as an artist in the United States ever since earning a Master of Fine Arts at Yale University in 1985. Born in Tokushima, Japan, she was an active member of the Tokyo art community prior to moving to the United States. She has exhibited widely in the United States and Japan and currently teaches at the Massachusetts Institute of Technology.

Matthew Teitelbaum is a curator at the The Institute for Contemporary Art in Boston, Massachusetts. A graduate of the University of London's Courtauld Institute, he moved to Boston from his position as curator at the Mendel Art Gallery in Saskatoon, Saskatchewan. He has written for Canadian and American art-related publications.

Bill Viola is a video artist living in the United States whose career has included travels to Italy, India, Indonesia, Tunisia, Japan and the South Pacific. He has been an artist-in-residence at the Sony Corporation in Japan and the San Diego Zoo. Among many others, an exhibition of his installations and videotapes was presented at the Museum of Modern Art in New York in 1987.

Laurie Walker is a Montreal-based artist who received her Master of Fine Art from the Nova Scotia College of Art and Design in 1987. Since her first solo exhibition at the Galerie Powerhouse in Montreal, she has exhibited across Canada.

Scott Watson is a Vancouver art historian, critic and writer who has contributed to numerous international art-related publications. His most recent book is entitled *Jack Shadbolt* (Douglas & McIntyre 1990). Prior to his current position as director/curator at the University of British Columbia Fine Arts Gallery, he was curator at the Vancouver Art Gallery.

Acknowledgements

This publication is inspired by a series of exhibitions at the Walter Phillips Gallery which were made possible through the generous support of the Canada Council and Alberta Art Foundation. We would like to extend special thanks to Reid Weir, who installed the challenging works in two of the exhibitions represented here, *Eye of Nature I* and *Eye of Nature II*, and Leslie Sampson who installed Christina Kubisch's *Landscapes*. Michael Toppings was a constant and reliable assistant for all three exhibitions, as was Bob Knowlden, whose skillful assistance was appreciated. Deborah Cameron, Media Complex staff and others at The Banff Centre have provided ongoing assistance in many ways and their support is always valued.

For the *Eye of Nature I* exhibition we would like to thank the artists, Bill Viola and Laurie Walker, for their dedication and insightful artworks. We are grateful for assistance from Galerie Christiane Chassay and generous loans from René Bertrand, Andrée and Patrice Drouin, Robert-Jean Chénier, Michel Giroux and the Newport Harbor Art Museum. Thanks are also extended to Brian Gray, chief preparator of the Newport Harbor Art Museum for his assistance with Bill Viola's installation.

We would like to thank Jeffrey Spalding and Ritsuko Taho, the artists in *Eye of Nature II* for their commitment to this project, and Alexander Birchler, Jill Armstrong and the Ceramics program at The Banff Centre for their special efforts toward Taho's installation. Generous loans from Diane Farris Gallery, Waddington and Shiell Galleries, and Eija Iris and Cecil Wishart are gratefully acknowledged.

To Christina Kubisch, we extend thanks for the energy and enthusiasm that she brought to her indoor and outdoor installations.

This publication is the product of the work of many people. We would like to thank Mary Anne Moser for her editorial input and skillful coordination of the project and Rik Zak and Barbara Sawchuk for their enthusiasm in conceiving the stimulating design. Engaging publication projects were created by Robert Fones, Rodney Graham, Carroll Moppett and Edward Poitras. Laurie Walker developed the endsheets, including twenty originals for special editions. It was a pleasure working with writers Hans Dickel, David Garneau, Maureen Sherlock, Matthew Teitelbaum and Scott Watson, whose incisive comments give depth and breadth to this investigation of cultural constructions of nature.

Daina Augaitis and Helga Pakasaar

WALTER PHILLIPS GALLERY
Box 1020
Banff Alberta
Canada T0L 0C0
(403) 762-6281

editors
Daina Augaitis and Helga Pakasaar

production and copy editor
Mary Anne Moser

designer
Sensetive In4mation

printer
Paperworks Press Limited

typographer
Paperwords

letterpress
Matrix Typesetters Ltd.

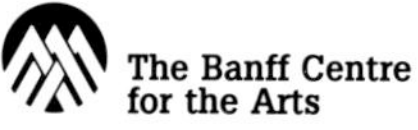

LXXVI. Among the different kinds of brambles is one called rhamnos by the Greeks, paler, more bushy, throwing out branches with straight thorns, not hooked like those of other brambles, and with larger leaves. The other kind of it is wild, darker and inclining to red, bearing a sort of pod. A decoction of the root of this in water makes a drug called lycium. *Lycium, etc.* The seed of it brings away the after-birth. The other, the paler kind, is more astringent, cooling, and more suitable for the treatment of gatherings and wounds. The leaves of either kind, raw or boiled, are made up into an ointment with oil.

LXXVII. A superior lycium may be made from the thorn which is also called [a] boxthorn, the characteristics of which are described [b] among Indian trees, for Indian is considered by far the best. The pounded branches or roots, which are of extreme bitterness, are boiled in water in a copper vessel for three days. The woody pieces are then taken away and the liquid boiled again until it is of the consistency of honey. It is adulterated with bitter juices, even with lees of olive oil and with ox gall. The froth, which may be called the flower of the decoction, is an ingredient of remedies for the eyes. The rest of the juice is used for clearing spots from the face and for the cure of itch, chronic fluxes of the eyes and corroding sores in their corners, pus in the ears, sore tonsils and gums, cough and spitting of blood. For these a piece the size of a bean is swallowed, or if there is discharge from wounds it is applied locally, as it is to chaps, ulcers of the genitals, excoriations, fresh, spreading and also festering ulcers, excrescences in the nostrils and suppurations. It is also taken in milk by women for excessive men-

These endsheets were created by
Laurie Walker and relate to her work
Wandering Bower (Solanum planetum) 1989
a drawing and sculpture installation.
Photo: the artist

laurel leaf, beeswax, iron oxide pigment,
pages from Pliny's *Natural History*
Photos: Denis Farley